WELLS

A SMALL CITY

WELLS

A SMALL CITY

Tony Scrase

TEMPUS

To my Aunt Nin

First published 2006

Tempus Publishing Limited
The Mill, Brimscombe Port,
Stroud, Gloucestershire, GL5 2QG
www.tempus-publishing.com

© Tony Scrase, 2006

The right of Tony Scrase to be identified as the Author
of this work has been asserted in accordance with the
Copyrights, Designs and Patents Act 1988.

British Library Cataloguing in Publication Data.
A catalogue record for this book is available from the British Library.

ISBN 0 7524 3595 7

Typesetting and origination by Tempus Publishing Limited
Printed in Great Britain

CONTENTS

ACKNOWLEDGEMENTS

My thanks are due to all of the following: at UWE, to the Faculty of the Built Environment for aid with illustrations and, within the Faculty, to Jan Major for help with things computer-orientated, to Simon Spokes for photographs and especially to Paul Revell for producing maps and diagrams from my scribbles; to successive generations of archivists at Wells Town Hall, Wells Cathedral and the Somerset County Record Office, and to the staff of the Somerset Studies Library for their unfailing help over a period of a quarter of a century; to all those at Wells who have corresponded with me and shared the results of their own studies, notably Richard Brookhead the late Linzee Colchester, Anne Duncan, Joan Hasler, the late Dr R.D. Reid and Tony Nott; to Tanya Bagwell at the Historical Environment Group, Somerset County Council; to Peter Kemmis Betty, Tom Sunley and Fran Gannon at Tempus Publishing; and lastly, in chronological order only, to my cousin Jill Struthers for help with proofs.

Acknowledgements for illustrations are due to Professor Mick Aston for the cover photograph and *colour plate 2*; R.K. Blencowe for *42*; the Courtauld Institute of Art, Lee of Fareham Collection for *colour plate 20*; Dr Warwick Rodwell for *5* and *colour plate 3*; the Somerset Archaeological and Natural History Society for *20*; the Historical Environment Group, Somerset County Council for *colour plates 6, 8, 13* and *14*; the Faculty of the Built Environment, UWE for *colour plates 5, 15* and *19*; and to the Cathedral Chapter of Wells for *colour plates 9* and *23*.

ABBREVIATIONS
AND OTHER USAGE

CB	Convocation Act Books, first of Wells Town Guild and then of Wells Corporation, Wells Town Hall archives
CPR	*Calendar of Patent Rolls* HMSO, London, 1901-2006
HMC WELLS	Historical Manuscripts Commission *Calendar of the Manuscripts of the Dean and Chapter of Wells*, 2 vols., HMSO, London 1907 & 1914
OS	Ordnance Survey
PRO	National Archives (formerly Public Record Office)
SANHS	Somerset Archaeological and Natural History Society
SRO	Somerset Record Office
SRS	Somerset Record Society
The Liberty	The Liberty of St Andrew
WCA	Wells Cathedral archives
WNHAS	Wells Natural History and Archaeological Society

The use of 'the Liberty' to denote the Liberty of St Andrew around the cathedral creates a possible ambiguity as that area contains today a street also called the Liberty. This has been distinguished as its two arms are described by former names as East Liberty and North Liberty. Otherwise modern street names have been used with three exceptions. They are firstly the western end

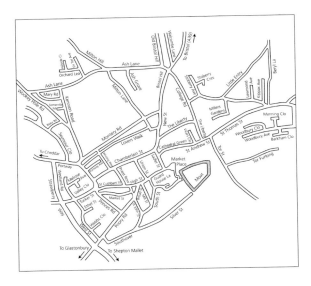

1 Modern street names

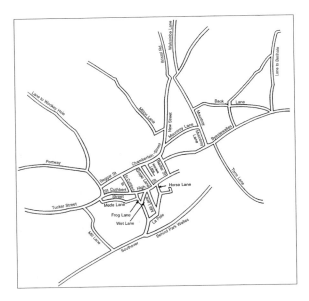

2 Street names, c.1400

of Chamberlain Street where the earlier name of Beggar Street indicates its very different character to the remainder of the street. Secondly, Mede Lane is used for Market Street to stress that this was originally a back lane and had nothing to do with markets until the cattle market was re-sited in the late nineteenth century. Finally, Wet Lane is used for the much narrower pre-1830 predecessor to Broad Street. However, for those who wish to know more on former and current usage, figures 1 and 2 show the modern situation and that of c.1400.

I

THE PHYSICAL SETTING

Wells is situated on a relatively narrow bench that separates the two major physical features of the area, the Mendip Hills and the Somerset Moors or Levels. Visually the high steep-sided plateau of Mendip is dominant (*colour plate 1*). It consists mainly of Carboniferous limestone but the formation is an eroded dome that reveals in places an older core. Some of this is volcanic material of Silurian age but it is mainly of Old Red Sandstone. The sandstone forms the highest area rising to 325m (1,025ft) at Blackdown. It also provides sharp scenic contrasts with acid-loving plants such as bracken and surface drainage as against the lime tolerant plants and swallets of the limestone. The limestone forms a plateau area with a fairly uniform surface at about 250m (810ft) above sea level. The whole system has been subjected to faulting and thrusting. This is particularly marked to the east of Wells. West Mendip presents a uniform and impressive face to the lower lands. East of Wells the face is broken and a series of outlying ridges give rise to Worminster Sleight, Dulcote and Lyatt Hills (*3*).

Subsequently, late Triassic and Liassic rocks were laid on the flanks of Mendip and to varying degrees over its surface. Patches of these remain on the higher ground but they are mainly significant as the bedrock of the Mendip foot bench. However, they are often overlaid by Head, a solifluction deposit of the Ice Age. This and Dolomitic Conglomerate, an earlier erosion material of the Triassic period, give fertile soils. These together with abundant springs and a

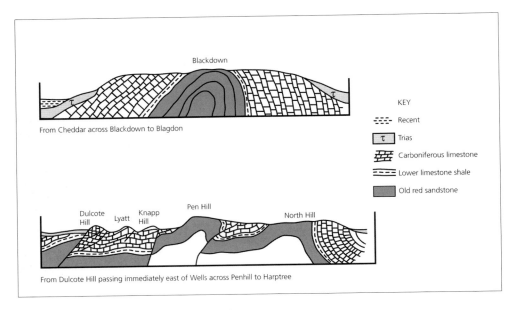

Blackdown

From Cheddar across Blackdown to Blagdon

KEY

- - - Recent

τ Trias

Carboniferous limestone

- - - Lower limestone shale

Old red sandstone

Pen Hill

Dulcote Hill   Lyatt   Knapp Hill   North Hill

From Dulcote Hill passing immediately east of Wells across Penhill to Harptree

3 Generalised cross sections across the Mendips

sheltered southern aspect, make the bench especially favourable for agriculture. It carried vineyards in the Middle Ages and has been famous for strawberries more recently.

To the south and west lie the Levels which do not exceed 7m (23ft) above sea level. The surface is broken only by a few chains of low hills and by 'island' sites such as Glastonbury and Wedmore. The geology is recent, comprising peat and bands of estuarine clay which represent marine transgressions. The whole area apart from the low hills was regularly flooded until modern drainage works. Even today episodes of local flooding occur periodically.

Sites on the bench have a number of potential advantages. They are above the flood lands but below the bleak top of Mendip. They are also in an excellent position to exploit the resources of the three contrasting zones. This economic potential is increased by the mineral wealth of the Mendips. The silver, lead and zinc ores are best known but there is also iron, fuller's earth, lime and a variety of building stones. Fuller's earth was significant in the development of the medieval textile industry at Wells. In addition the Levels offered peat as either a fuel or an agricultural aid.

Wells had specific advantages from its location at the transition to the heavily faulted eastern Mendips. Firstly, the thrusting gave an easy ascent eastwards on to the plateau. St Thomas Street represents the first stage of this route that led to the Fosse Way and eventually to Frome (*4*). An east/west route on this alignment may

4 The landscape setting. This view is from Tor Hill looking across the modern extensions on the east of Wells to the main mass of the Mendips. It shows how the town is both constrained by its setting and how it is seen with a series of attractive natural backdrops

well have provided the early spine of the settlement. Secondly, the geological disturbances had, in effect, trapped a considerable volume of ground water and diverted it to the great spring at Wells. The insertion of dyes into swallets has revealed that the spring draws on sources extending in a quadrant from Pen Hill above Wells to Beacon Hill above Shepton Mallet. This means that this spring is particularly large and vigorous. It has therefore drawn human attention from early periods onwards.

However, Wells lacked one natural advantage. Its streams were adequate to drive mills but were too small to be made navigable. The town would thus have to rely on more expensive land transport systems throughout the Middle Ages and Early Modern periods. This was to put it at a disadvantage compared with its main rivals in Somerset which were Bath, Bridgwater and Taunton.

2

BEFORE THE CATHEDRAL

PREHISTORY

Wells is in an area with a long history of human occupation. So it is to be expected that people were moving across what was to be the city from early times. Palaeolithic remains are found along the flanks of Mendip but none has yet been discovered at Wells. However, the modern excavation in the Camery did reveal Mesolithic flints amongst the 1,773 flakes found.

As populations began to farm and became more settled, evidence becomes abundant around Wells. In the Neolithic there were long barrows and Priddy Circles on Mendip and the earliest trackways on the Levels. By the Iron Age there were hillforts on Mendip and the lake village by Glastonbury. Obviously, such populations must have exploited the bench but hillwash, continual cultivation and building activity have obliterated much evidence. In the immediate vicinity of Wells there are only a few sites or finds. In 1941 an anti-tank trench was dug across the Bishop's Park towards Coxley. At the Coxley end it produced a Neolithic macehead. There is rather more from the Iron Age. A typical promontory enclose known as King's Castle is located on Tor Hill and links up with a 'Celtic' field system on Lyatt Hill.

ROMAN TIMES

Occupation of the area must have intensified as the Romans exploited the minerals of Mendip. Given their religious practices it would be surprising if such a major spring had not attracted at least a shrine. The excavation in the Camery produced evidence. Over 200 sherds, glass and bronze fragments were found. There were also building remains including Roman concrete which would not travel far from its source. The distribution led Dr. Warwick Rodwell to postulate a building to the north or north-west. This probably means it is under the cathedral and inaccessible. Within the excavated area he found the remains of a late-Roman mausoleum with two phases of work (5 and 6). This structure can be related to a number of Roman finds in the area. The first museum curator, Herbert Balch, found a Roman coin in the garden while the anti-tank trench produced pottery, including Samian ware, a lead cup south of Park Wood and more pottery and a fibula towards Coxley. Between 2000 and 2003 archaeological evaluations and observation have indicated that there was Romano-British occupation in the Southover area.

We have two possible names for this Roman settlement. This profusion probably results from churchmen, chroniclers and historians trying rather too

5 The beginning of the sequence in the Camery. The excavation in the Camery revealed these remains of a Roman mausoleum which was to effect subsequent developments. *Courtesy Dr Warwick Rodwell*

hard to find some early roots. One name is Theodorodunum. It is given in Camden's *Britannia* with an attribution to John Leland. Unfortunately, it must have been in those parts of Leland's papers lost before the eighteenth century. It seems a doubtful form. Most surviving Romano-British place names are of British origins. British names lacked a *th* sound and it only occurs in Latin in loan words from Greek. The other two elements could be known British forms. *Duro* means a lowland fort, often a Roman creation, while *duno* is a hillfort. Normally they are alternatives not linked. The more likely explanation is a later creation anachronistically linking the name Theodore and a known Romano-British final element. The second name is Fontanetum. This occurs in various medieval sources and seems to derive from a Glastonbury charter, the so-called *Magnum Privilegium Inae Regis*. The charter is clearly a forgery. It purports to limit the bishop's power over the abbey. Unfortunately, in Ine's day the bishop would have been in Winchester until 705 and later in Sherbourne not in Wells. But like many forgeries it copied genuine early material so it has ancient names such as Lantocai. So the question is whether Fontanetum could be of this type. It certainly resembles provincial names in Gaul, but it is from Latin and there is no similar British form in the 400 names in standard Roman lists such as the Ptolomey's Geography, the Antonine Itinerary or the *Notitia Dignitum*. Neither name nor anything approximating to them appears in these.

THE EARLY MIDDLE AGES 410–905

There is surprisingly little trace of British activity in the centuries between the Roman withdrawal and incorporation into Wessex. Place names with British elements or naming Celtic saints are common elsewhere in Somerset but not here. Only four can be found in the large manor of Wells. Keward on the south-west of the town has some early spellings of *Kuer* suggesting a British element giving names such as Curry Mallet or Curry Rivet elsewhere. Priddy probably relates to the Welsh for earth while Church Hill on the eastern boundary is one of those anomalous churchill names that never had a church and comes from Old Welsh *cruc* meaning a hillock. The pen in Pen Hill is Welsh or Cornish for hill.

The earliest documentary evidence is a grant of 766 of land around Wellow to the minster church 'next to the great spring called Wielea'. However, the early histories of the diocese reach back further. They are three, beginning with the *Historiola* written soon after 1174. The others, the *Historia Minor* and the *Historia Major*, are found in the Wells Register, the *Liber Albus II*. They date to after 1367 and 1408 respectively. They agree that King Ine founded the minster church around 700. The *Historiola* has a story of him transferring a Celtic bishopric

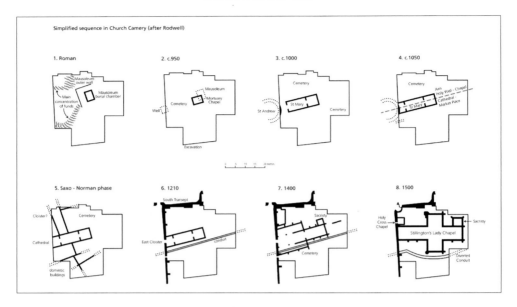

6 Simplified sequence in Church Camery (after Rodwell)

from Congresbury. This was probably an attempt to keep up with the even more remarkable pretensions of Glastonbury. They also have a claimed original name of Anglo-Saxon type. The *Historiola* has the town formerly called Cideston, now Wells. This is perhaps a copyist's error as the writer of the *Historia Minor* uses the earlier source and has Tydeston instead. The name must relate to the reference to 'Wells formerly called Tidington' in a forged charter allegedly of Edward the Confessor. Attempts to relate these names to later medieval field names like Tithesput or Tydesbury are not very convincing. The location of Tideston and its significance in settlement terms remains unclear.

It is a relief to turn to the clearer facts of archaeology. The mausoleum was obviously still apparent. Its north/south orientation might indicate pagan origins but it had gained Christian associations. It became a focus for Anglo-Saxon burials. St Andrew's Well, the mausoleum and the minster church seem to have formed an axial group (*6* and *colour plates 3* and *4*).

A minster was a church that provided religious facilities to a large territory in the days of before parish provision. There is no sign that Wells ever had a monastic organisation but we do not know where its priests lived or how many people served them. Presumably, all were nearby. Certainly, the Out Parish of St Cuthbert's, the largest in Somerset, is a relic of the minster's sphere of influence.

3

CATHEDRAL STATUS AND TOWN ORIGINS 909-1242

In 909 King Edward reorganised the Wessex dioceses. The large bishopric of Sherbourne was divided into units based on the local counties. Wells was selected as the centre for Somerset. The reasons for this choice are unclear. Certainly, it was conveniently placed towards the centre of the shire in contrast to Bath or Ilchester. But this could have been claimed for other sites notably nearby Glastonbury or Cheddar. Obviously, the Anglo-Saxon state saw no need to concentrate functions. In this locality the *burh* (the fortification and trading centre) was at Axbridge, the palace and seat of royal administration at Cheddar and the main church at Wells.

The consequences of this choice were many. Wells gained an important new household and it was one that was to grow in consequence as more estates were granted to the bishop over the following centuries. This would have increased population and the demand for skills necessary to serve them. It would also have drawn people to Wells on estate business. The status of cathedral must have necessitated improvements or a total rebuilding of the church. It was only after 909 that the mausoleum was filled in after final use as an ossuary. It was followed by a mortuary chapel which covered some pre-existing burials presumably of special significance. Later this was enlarged to a two-cell building, the eastern portion of which corresponded closely to the mortuary chapel. This was done by Bishop Giso's time (1061–88) as he endowed St Mary's Chapel, and we know that this was the name of the structure. By his time a vestibule linked it to the apse of the cathedral which was just apparent projecting beyond the later cloisters. Buildings were also added to the south and north, perhaps as part of Giso's communal buildings (*6*).

The cathedral's dignity and specialised functions would have suggested the need for a separate church for local inhabitants. At some stage a church and chapel were provided. Their dedications are clearly Anglo-Saxon, being as they were to St Cuthbert and St Etheldreda. These are not names which would have readily occurred to a Norman bishop and the need would have faded when Bishop John moved his seat to Bath. However, there is no hard evidence. The present structure of the parish church of St Cuthbert is Early English or later, apart from a Norman pillar piscina. Documentation dates to after 1200 with one exception. Again the exact significance of the two additional churches is unclear. Did they serve separate hamlets? Perhaps St Cuthbert's was for the lay servants and craftsmen serving the cathedral and its staff while St Etheldreda served the agricultural workers. Alternatively could either have originated, like many parish churches, as the house chapel of one of the bishop's thanes?

Early history is obscure. Many of the bishops are little more than names although we do know that several had been monks at Glastonbury. Rodwell argues on the strength of the Lanalet Pontifical (an Anglo-Saxon document preserved at Rouen) that a cathedral may have been consecrated in the first half of the eleventh century. The last two Anglo-Saxon appointments were continentals. Canute appointed Dudoc an Old-Saxon while Edward the Confessor selected Giso from Liège diocese in modern Belgium to succeed him. It is during Giso's time that we begin to get a clearer picture of the settlement.

It is certain that the basic road pattern of the town, as defined by High Street on the south and Chamberlain Street on the north with four links between them (*2*), was orientated on the Anglo-Saxon cathedral rather than its Gothic successor. High Street is aligned with, and blocked by, the west end of the first cathedral. However, the significance of this is disputed. Amongst recent commentators Rodwell argues for market functions by late Anglo-Saxon times while David Shaw maintained that the town was a creation of the twelfth century.

GISO'S WELLS 1061–88

We know more of Wells during Giso's time for two reasons. Firstly, the *Historiola* incorporates what seems to be a fragment of his autobiography. Secondly, his episcopate includes the time of the Domesday survey. Thanks to Domesday's documentation of both the time of King Edward and 'now' we can see how his lands changed after the Conquest.

Giso was not impressed by what he found. A 'mediocre church' was staffed by four or five priests who lived in the wider community and had to beg for their bread. This last statement presumably meant that they relied on voluntary offerings. He reordered the conditions of the priests, establishing a communal life with their own refectory and dormitory. He also settled them on some property so that they had an income of about £20 per annum by 1086. A provost managed their estates while an archdeacon supervised the services. The number of canons increased to perhaps ten.

The bishop's estates had been growing steadily but by 1061 they were attracting the greedy eye of the Earl of Wessex, the future Harold II. After his defeat some were returned immediately but the best, Congresbury, was not regained until later. Giso also obtained further estates. By 1086 he was worth about £200. It was a comfortable sum but not in the first rank of Church estates.

Domesday tells us about the manor of Wells, but what relates to the core settlement and what relates to the hamlets is debatable. Our view will depend on what weight we attach to our second doubtful charter. This purported grant of Edward the Confessor must have been produced to safeguard the bishop's holdings. It certainly contains authentic material and lists all the hamlets. So Wells may have composed of one cluster of houses near the cathedral, another by St Cuthbert's and a third in Southover. The entry gives no signs of urban activity. However, it is concerned with which places paid dues to the king and the Somerset entries are weak on towns. Some places are listed with burgesses but no market while others only have a market mentioned.

Certainly, the manor was rich and the bishop's four mills are likely to have included what later became the town mills, and were known as inmills and outmills. Between 1066 and 1086 the bishop established three knights on his lands to fulfil his military duties to the king. All had holdings elsewhere in Somerset. For example, Erneis held Downhead from Glastonbury Abbey, land at Evercreech from the bishop and land at Bruton from Roger of Courseulles. As we shall see knight's holdings characterised the early town and the link with Downhead certainly persisted.

THE BISHOPS AT BATH 1088-1206

Giso was succeeded by John variously called de Villula, of Tours or the Physician. He transferred his seat to Bath. Ostensibly this was in accordance with the

Conqueror's decree that bishops should be based in towns not villages. But there were other reasons behind this move. John obtained the Abbey of Bath (and turned out most of the monks) and purchased the town from William Rufus. Given his interest in medicine the hot springs may have also attracted him. He was as harsh with the Wells canons as with the Bath monks. Their communal buildings were demolished and they were turned out to live 'in common with the people'. There was worse to come. John's brother and steward, Heldebert, was made provost and granted at least £30 of the church's revenues. He then paid each canon £3 per annum. John had a house built on the site of the communal buildings. Probably, his brother lived there.

Wells had lost the bishop and his household. This must have impoverished such craftsmen and traders as may have been present. However, the canons would have needed more servants individually than as a single community. Some things probably continued though, most notably a school and choristers. Also the lack of a resident lord may have left room for enterprise. By Robert of Lewes' time the settlement possessed three fairs. They were either relics of Anglo-Saxon activity or had emerged in the bishop's absence.

Heldebert's possessions and office passed to his heirs. John's successor, Bishop Godfrey (1122-35) made an unsuccessful attempt to regain them. However, it was the next bishop, Robert of Lewes (1135-66), who transformed the situation. He was a close supporter of King Stephen. This no doubt strengthened his hand in dealing with Heldebert's second heir, Reginald. In return for the post of precentor and the use of the manor of Combe, Reginald was persuaded to surrender lands sufficient to support several canons. Stipends were increased from £3 to £5.

Bishop Robert gave the church a new, cathedral-like, constitution. These Statutes' were first authorised early in Robert's episcopate but survive in a fifteenth-century copy which includes later amendments dating until at least 1159. The canons were now headed by a dean. He was one of the *quinque personae*, who formed the main government. The others were the precentor who was responsible for music, the treasurer, the archdeacon of Wells and the chancellor. The last had charge of books, records and the school. The dean and precentor were given deputies, the subdean and the succentor respectively. The Statutes provisions for both a school and choristers seem to show that both had survived John's departure.

Robert also did something about the church's fabric. What was involved is obscure. However, it was radical enough to call for a reconsecration and dedication in 1148. But if it was a total reconstruction it seems surprising that his successor should start again before 1180.

Finally, he granted the first town charter to Wells although it may have been inspired by his reorganisation of the church. Unfortunately, it does not survive and we know it by what was repeated in later charters. Certainly, one of his motives was to banish the fairs, from the church and its courtyard, into the town's 'broad places'. These pre-existing fairs were held on the feasts of the Invention of the Cross in May, St Calixtus in October and St Andrew in November. These were major Church festivals when people came to pray and stayed to trade. They are amongst the earliest recorded fairs in England. Robert increased their length to three days each. He set out boundaries for his borough and granted burgess status to the townsfolk. This freed them from feudal dues and labour. They owed the bishop an annual rent of 12d for their burgage. In return they were free to sell, give or bequeath it. Similarly, they could come and go without permission. They were also given a monopoly in the trade in hides and fells.

His successor Bishop Reginald (1174-91) issued no less than three charters. Two confirmed Robert's grants of burgage tenure and the fairs. The first was stated to have been done on the petition of the burgesses of Wells. This indicates that citizens had some sort of collective voice. His final charter outlined new boundaries to allow for growth. The extension seems to have added Southover to the borough (Peacock 2000 2-6).

Reginald also began the rebuilding of St Andrew's as a Gothic church. The new structure was laid out to the north of the Anglo-Saxon cathedral. It is just possible that it replaced an unfinished Romanesque building commenced by Robert but it is more likely that Norman cloisters were demolished. It was on an obviously different alignment (by 12°) to the old church and therefore to the town. The first stage of the new building was a Lady chapel and the quire. These were complete by 1184. Work then began on the transepts and this phase continued until about the time of Bishop Savaric's death in 1205. By c.1190 the Anglo-Saxon church had been demolished. Soon after work started on the eastern arm of the cloisters. The original intention was for a square of cloisters and the eastern range was initially narrower than today (7) (Rodwell 2001 245-308).

Others features are documented from Reginald's time. Canon's Barn is mentioned around 1175 and we can name the schoolmaster, Peter de Winton, c.1188. In addition more prebends were being created. At about this time the chapel in Southover gained an altar to St Thomas (Becket) and from that time is often referred to as St Thomas' Chapel.

The main gap in our knowledge of these years concerns motives. We do not know why Bishops Robert and Reginald invested so much effort and money in Wells. The initial attempt to regain property alienated to Heldebert's family is understandable, but why did they do so much more?

The next bishop, Savaric (1192-1205), had many other things to concern him. He was employed on government business, notably in negotiating Richard I's release. He obtained the abbotship of Glastonbury and changed his title to

7 The doorway from the south
transept to the east cloister.
Obviously it was designed
to be seen, but subsequent
decisions to widen the cloister
and to add an upper storey
have left it partly obscured and
off centre

Bishop of Bath and Glastonbury. This involved him in a bitter struggle with the
monks of Glastonbury. Nevertheless, he found time to take an interest in Wells,
if only as a source of prestige and income. By 1201 he granted the town another
charter reiterating previous grants and adding a fourth fair on the morrow of St
John the Baptist in June. He set out the borough bounds but did this by copying
both Robert's limits and Reginald's extension which is confusing in the south-
west section. Also, two of his landmarks were where crosses had formerly stood.

He obtained a confirmation from King John in 1201. John's charter mentions
a weekly market for the first time although it was clearly already in existence.
He added two new privileges. The town was recognised as a free town with free
burgages, so the bishop could not revoke that status. Also, he granted a fifth fair
to be held in May on the Translation of St Andrew and lasting for eight days. In
70 years the days for fairs had grown from three to twenty.

John was probably in Wells at the time as he personally held the assizes there in that year. It is a measure of its importance that it could by then accommodate the king and those attending.

Work also continued on the new church. By 1196 there was the first of a series of changes of plan for the cloisters. It was decided to preserve the ancient chapel of St Mary. This meant that an unorthodox site would be needed for the chapter house.

BISHOP JOSCELIN'S WELLS 1206–42

The new bishop was a native of Wells manor and quickly returned the seat of the bishop to the town. There were sound practical reasons for doing so. It was a more central location for the diocese and its urban status was now clear. He abandoned Savaric's struggles with Glastonbury and dropped that part of his title in 1219.

Joscelin's main impact on Wells was delayed for some years. He was one of the bishops who in 1208 served the Interdict on King John and the next year went into exile with his brother Hugh, who had been elected bishop of Lincoln but not yet consecrated. They returned in 1213. In fact, Joscelin and Hugh seem to have been on good terms with John. When Hugh was still archdeacon of Wells he was in the royal service. John gave him the manor and palace at Cheddar and from him it passed to Joscelin and his successors.

Under Joscelin building continued on the new church. The eastern part of the nave was commenced in 1205 and continued in Joscelin's early years. This campaign extended the nave west to the position of the North Porch. It was completed by 1210 when the bishop was in exile and work came to a halt. When it resumed there were changes. Some were matters of style and techniques. Most obviously, some new hoist or wheel had become available and blocks of stone were larger. However, there was also a change of plan. The west front was now to be deeply buttressed (*colour plate 5*). This in turn necessitated changes to the cloisters. Eventually the west and south ranges were built wider than the east range but the north range was abandoned. Finally, in 1239 St Andrew's was consecrated afresh. Work then commenced on the chapter house complex, involving the outside walls of the undercroft and the stairs. But the dispute about elections that followed Joscelin's death and the resulting reference to Rome brought work to a halt. Funds were dissipated and major work halted for 40 years although minor operations continued on the west front and cloisters.

Joscelin needed an appropriate home so the first part of the palace, the eastern range, was built in his time. It featured a first-floor hall over a crypt. He also

8 The north-eastern corner of the Bishop's Park. The old road to Shepton Mallet now runs along the edge of the woodland and has to climb across the flank of Tor Hill. Prior to the eastward extension of the park the road followed the lower ground at the foot of the hill. In the early nineteenth century this section of the park was planted with specimen trees in the manner of a landscape garden

provided other features appropriate for a great household. In 1207 he received two permissions from the king relating to a deer park. The first licensed the park and permitted him to divert the road through the wood towards Wellesleigh. The second pushed the boundaries outwards. On the west he was allowed to divert the Glastonbury road and on the east the road under Tor Hill towards 'Dultingcote'. Presumably, this second must have moved the Shepton Mallet road east from a previous crossroads with East Liberty and St Andrew Street to create Tor Street. The creation of the park had a profound impact on the settlement. The steep slope of Mendip limited expansion northwards. Now the park stopped growth southward. Wells was forced to extend on an east/west axis, giving it an elongated form which has characterised it ever since (*8* and *colour plate 1*).

The area around the cathedral was also beginning to assume a more familiar form as the increasing number of prebends was reflected through an increase in canonical houses (*9*). The grants of several survive. Nicholas de Well' gave the house opposite the great door of St Andrew's which was presumably the modern Music School. Hugh gave its neighbour which could be the museum or the site of Vicars' Close. The east side of College Road and East Liberty was dominated

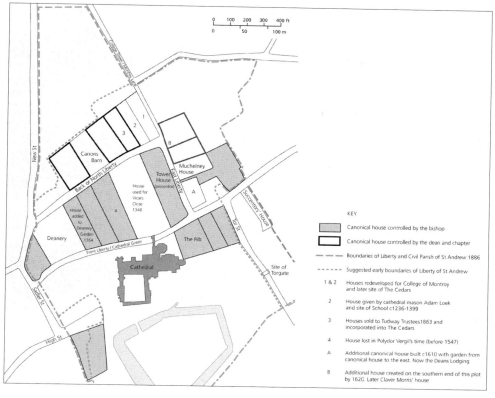

KEY

▨	Canonical house controlled by the bishop
▢	Canonical house controlled by the dean and chapter
— — —	Boundaries of Liberty and Civil Parish of St Andrew 1886
- - - -	Suggested early boundaries of Liberty of St Andrew
1 & 2	Houses redeveloped for College of Montroy and later site of The Cedars
2	House given by cathedral mason Adam Loek and site of School c1236-1399
3	Houses sold to Tudway Trustees1863 and incorporated into The Cedars
4	House lost in Polydor Vergil's time (before 1547)
A	Additional canonical house built c1610 with garden from canonical house to the east. Now the Deans Lodging
B	Additional house created on the southern end of this plot by 1620. Later Claver Morris' house

9 The canonical houses

*c.*1200 by two large properties owned by Walter de Dunheved (Downhead) and John de Kardunvilla. To the south was the croft of Adam Giwold and, on the corner, a pear orchard. Some of the earliest deeds surviving show the large properties of Walter and John being divided up, coming into clerical hands and being granted for use by a canon. Also in this period the three properties on the site of the Cedars (15 North Liberty) were given, as was the succentor's house at 8 and 8a St Thomas Street. The outcome was a series of at least 16 canonical houses for those, of what became over 50 canons, who had to live in Wells. However, the central house on the Cedars site was quickly diverted to become a site for the school (*9*).

This wider area of priestly accommodating beyond the actual cathedral precinct formed the Liberty of St Andrew. As a result the built-up area had three units. On the west was the borough which also formed the In Parish of St Cuthbert. In the centre was the Liberty, which was part of the city but had separate administrative and judicial arrangements. Also its residents worshipped

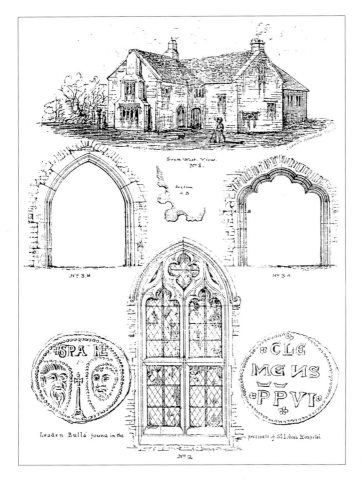

10 St John's Hospital. This is Serel's recording of the main buildings at the time of their demolition to make way for the new Central School. Besides a general view he sketched some architectural details and finds

in the cathedral rather than St Cuthbert's. On the east was Byestwalles (or East Wells by 1550) which was a suburb and formed part of the bishop's manor and Out Parish. To complicate matters the bounds of the Liberty were adjusted several times. When illustrated on the 1886 OS map they carefully exclude the Fountain Inn. Earlier adjustments had excluded the garden of the Market Place canonical house when it was developed, and the succentor's house when that office was merged with the dean or subdean and the property became the Goat Inn. These adjustments created an anomalous strip on the east. It was in the city and Parliamentary borough but not subject to borough government or courts.

The holdings of the knightly Dunheved and Kardunvilla families should be noted. In fact Walter had also owned what became the succentor's house. Slightly later transactions show that two other knights had holdings in High Street. Obviously, it was convenient for them to have a base in Wells at this time.

Joscelin and Hugh also provided a hospital for the town. It was in Southover, adjoining the millstream where there must have been a gap between the main built-up area and the houses of Southover. This hospital had a prior and ten brothers. It is often dismissed as a minor house but this is unfair. It became the second largest property owner in the borough and had lands elsewhere. It maintained a decent number of brothers throughout its existence and still had ten in 1377 after Black Death. It was ultimately dissolved in 1539 along with the larger monasteries (*10*).

On Joscelin's death the monks of Bath proceeded to elect Roger of Salisbury as bishop without consulting the canons of Wells and in defiance of Henry III. The matter was referred to the Pope. Innocent IV issued a Bull establishing future organisation of the diocese. It required future bishops to take the title of Bath and Wells. Joint elections were to be mandatory. Wells renewed cathedral status was clear. Roger was buried at Bath but he was not to be joined by another bishop (James Montague) for nearly four centuries. Wells had resumed its position of the heart of the diocese.

4

SUCCESS DESPITE CRISES
1242–1400

Whatever the true sequence of its origins, Wells was a functioning and successful urban centre by the second half of the thirteenth century. This can be demonstrated in a number of ways. The physical extent was already broadly what it was to be until after 1830. All the major streets are documented prior to 1300. The early documentation also reveals a good range of occupations. We can disregard the many priests and the rural-sounding parker and vine grower. Similarly the masons and plumber may well have been employed at the cathedral or palace. Beyond these we get the range to be expected in any small town: butchers, bakers and cooks; shoemakers and cobblers; and smiths. In addition the textile trades are already well represented with a fell or hide dealer, a number of tuckers or fullers, a dyer, weaver and hosier. In addition one street is specifically named for tuckers and there were references to fulling mills as early as Bishop Joscelin's time. There are also signs of larger-scale operations and demands for more luxurious goods in the presence of a goldsmith, a spicier, a mercer and a merchant. Some citizens were wealthy enough to leave property to the Church for the good of their souls.

All this must have been helped when the bishop was a great officer of state, as was the case with Robert Burnell. When he entertained orders must have poured out to town traders. The great hall he built at the palace demonstrates the scale of his household and hospitality. Interestingly, the hall is on the alignment of the Anglo-Saxon church suggesting that it replaced Bishop John's manor house.

The pace of work gradually picked up on the cathedral. In around 1260 the northern part of the east cloister was widened and accommodation provided over it. Subsequently, work resumed on the chapter house.

THE EARLY FOURTEENTH CENTURY

The century began badly. The climate was deteriorating from the previous warm phase. The initial sign was a series of disastrous summers from 1311 to 1319. Crops failed but problems went beyond the immediate crisis. The population growth of the previous two centuries meant that agriculture was over-stretched. Too much land had been under the plough for too long a period with too little fertiliser. Soil structures were at risk. Blanket bogs began to grow and agriculture retreated from higher ground. By 1315 there was famine and the whole economy suffered. However, there were signs of recovery by the mid-1320s.

While some Somerset towns such as Ilchester, Milbourne Port and Stogursey obviously suffered it is difficult to find signs of this at Wells. Documentation increases rapidly, particularly as regards property. This was because of pious bequests. People were anxious to hurry their passage through purgatory. This could be achieved by good works or the prayers of the faithful. If you were a great lord you might endow an abbey and thus obtain the prayers of generations of monks. Founding a hospital or almshouse was both a good work and earned you the prayers of future residents, but only bishops managed this at medieval Wells. A rich merchant might aspire to a chantry in a major church and leave money to employ a priest to pray for him daily. Distribution of bread to the poor was considered another good work that could be undertaken. More ordinary folk might leave a rent to secure themselves an obit, an annual commemoration service. Those who could not afford this could join a guild which would hire a priest to pray for past and present members. In Wells property came into the hands of all of the cathedral, the Hospital of St John and the parish church for these purposes (*11*). The associated documents were preserved and the archives concerning the cathedral and parish church are our main source. The records of the hospital were lost at the Reformation but something can be inferred from the mortmain licenses obtained from the Crown to permit alienation to the Church. These also show that religious bodies from outside began to obtain property in the town. In 1306 Thomas de Berkeley paid £5 for a license to permit him to grant two High Street properties (modern 18 and 20) to the nunnery of Minchen Buckland (*11*).

From these property records we discover increasing pressure to settle in Wells. Property on main streets was divided into small units, some merely a small shop

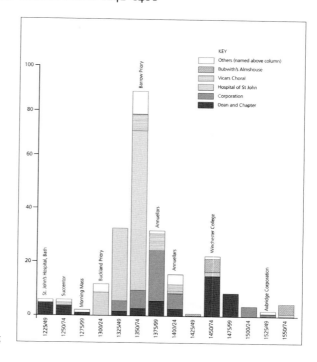

11 Patterns of giving

with a solar over. Houses began to appear along Mede Lane (modern Market Street) which had been purely a back lane to property on St Cuthbert and High Streets. Also the number of persons who could afford these pious bequests was increasing. However, it may be a symptom of problems that for the first three quarters of the century, the main beneficiary was the hospital.

The records also show an increasing diversity of trades in Wells. By 1350 when bynames were hardening into hereditary surnames (and can therefore no longer be used) some thirty-three trades had been noted. Bynames can also indicate place of origin. They reveal that over a third of townsfolk came from within 10 miles and 61 per cent from within 25 miles. But others came from further afield; from Devon in the west, Scotland and Cumbria in the north, East Anglia in the east and France and the Low Countries to the southeast. This is more extensive than a typical market town but less than a major centre such as Winchester (Keene 1985 ii 373).

We have a chance to see Wells in a county context in 1327 as the Lay Subsidy records for Somerset survive. It was the second wealthiest town in the county with an assessed wealth of £201 compared with Bridgwater's £211. Bath was third with £165. Wells also had three of the richest town traders in the county with Thomas Testwode, Peter le Botoyr and Nicholas Camberlyn each paying £1 on goods worth £20. The only urban resident to exceed them was Sir Hugh de Courtenay at Crewkerne and he was a feudal magnate whose family became earls of Devon. Similarly the other payers of £1 at Castle Cary and South Petherton were lords of the manor. Only Taunton had one ordinary townsman paying £1. The wealthiest inhabitant of Bridgwater paid 18s and the counterpart for Bath paid 16s.

The payers were a small elite. Probably the 64 payers at Wells were no more than 3 per cent of the total population. Furthermore, within this group wealth was very unevenly distributed. The top three paid almost a third of the whole and the top third of payers had 79 per cent of the assessed wealth. This wealth was of course only calculated on movables, that is goods and cash. Property holdings reveal a somewhat different ranking although Thomas Testwode, with nine properties, is the most affluent by this count also. One other point about the payers is that Peter le Botoyr was French. As we shall see the leading merchant of the next generation was also French. These men must have been drawn to Wells by its trading opportunities.

Wells can also be placed in a regional and national context in 1334 as there are complete records for the subsidy of that year. This tax was done in a different way. Representatives of each 'vill' agreed an appropriate sum with two government nominees. It was then up to the place to decide how to raise it. The sums were employed without a new general assessment until 1524. Wells paid on wealth of £190 which probably reflects negotiating ability rather than any change in circumstances. It was still second wealthiest in Somerset, while it was twelfth in the south west and eighty-sixth nationally (*12*).

Somerset towns ranked by wealth		South Western towns and their national context	
1. Bridgwater **T**	£260	1. Bristol [2]	£2,200
2. **Wells T**	£190	2. Salisbury [12]	£750
3. Shepton Mallet	£158	3. Gloucester [17]	£540
4. Crewkerne	£144	4. Exeter [23]	£406
5. Castle Cary	£135	5. Plymouth [24]	£400
6. Bath **T**	£133	6. Marshfield [44]	£270
7. Frome	£130	7. Bridgwater [50]	£260
8. Taunton **T**	£102	8. Cirencester [52]	£250
9. Bruton	£95	9. Tewkesbury [59]	£243
10. Wincanton	£90	10. Ottery St Mary [79]	£200
11. South Petherton	£62	11. Shaftesbury [80]	£200
12. Somerton **T**	£59	12. **Wells** [86]	£190
13. Ilminster	£54	13. Barnstaple [87]	£187
14. Keynsham	£53	14. Painswick [88]	£186
15. Yeovil	£49	15. Truro [89]	£182

16. Axbridge **T**	£45	16. Bath [100]	£133
17. Ilchester★ **T**	£40		
= Langport **T**	£40		
19. Minehead	£38		
20. Milverton **T**	£35		
21. Dulverton	£32		
= Montacute **T**	£32		
23. Dunster **T**	£31		
24. Milborne Port **T**	£31		
25. North Petherton	£30		
26. Wellington	£22		
27. Stogursey **T**	£20		
28. Weare **T**	£14		
29. Chard **T**	£13		
30. Watchet **T**	£11		
31. Stoford **T**	£9		
32. Nether Stowey **T**	£7		
33. Newport	£6		

12 Wells in relation to other towns in 1334

Numbers on the left of column 2 are regional ranking. Numbers in square brackets national rankings after *Cambridge Urban History*

★ with part of Sock Denis assessed as *of Britain* I, pp. 755-7. ancient demesne. **T** paying a tenth

Wells actually paid rather more, as this subsidy took a tenth of the value of movables in boroughs, compared to the uniform twentieth of 1327. Wells was booming in these years so it is unlikely that its wealth had declined. Physical expansion continued up to the eve of the Black Death. In Tucker Street paddocks were being divided and laid out for houses and the tentering ranks on which fulled cloth was dried and stretched. The first permanent house in the middle of High Street was built in 1345. Rents were increasing. So it is improbable that its wealth was less than that of little Marshfield in Gloucestershire which was only founded *c.*1265. Instead it seems likely that Wells had citizens able to negotiate and exercise influence. One such was Peter le Monier, the first layman of whom we can draw a reasonably rounded picture. His career is another clue to rising prosperity in Wells.

Peter was French and from Amiens. He is first recorded in England in 1314/15 when he and his brother, James le Petit, established the latter's son Thomas as their agent in Exeter. Then in 1329 the Patent Rolls contain a grant. Peter, the son of James le Monoier of Amiens, was to be free of customs on wool, hides, wood and all other goods he imported or exported. He was also to be free of any arrest for debts except his own. This was granted because of 'the labours daily endured by William de Monte Acuto, dwelling at the king's side'. This makes no link with Wells but that followed in 1333 in the first of a series of brief safe conducts, 'Protection for one year for the king's merchant, Peter son of James le Monier, burgess of Wells for his men and goods'. The series continued until 1347 but it is worth quoting that of 1340 which is more detailed. It is a grant of two years safe conduct for:

> Peter le Moyner, who is by birth of the town of Amiens now a burgess of the town of Wells, having there a wife and children and a permanent domicile, paying lot and scot and other charges as a denizen and making continual stay within the realm and his goods and wares and men and servants; granted out of consideration for William de Monte Acuto, Earl of Salisbury, the said Peter being of his household and specially attendant on his business and that he may traffic about the realm as he will....

So Peter was a merchant of substance and well connected. Furthermore, in the year of the Battle of Sluys he had opted for England not France. However, we can only speculate as to Peter's services to the Earl of Salisbury. Was it as a merchant? It seems likely that it went further and involved the interrelated areas of diplomacy and espionage. However, he also had more straightforward trading activities and was exporting cloth through Bristol and Dartmouth in the 1340s.

In Wells Peter's career changed direction in 1343. He then began to invest in the local property market, probably because the early stages of the Hundred Years War had disrupted the wool and cloth trades and new outlets were needed for capital. The main result was the creation of Monier's Lane running south from Chamberlain Street in the area of the modern Catholic church. By this time his first wife was dead and there is no further mention of their children. In 1346 he remarried. His second wife was Margery, daughter and heiress of Thomas Testwode. She must have been much younger than Peter as she was to outlive him by some 40 years (Scrase 1989a 131-2; Shaw 1993 91; Kowaleski 1995 262). Peter's choice of Wells must be a testament to the significance of the town in these years.

While the town flourished works continued on the cathedral. The chapter house was finished by 1306 and the eastern Lady chapter by 1320. The quire was then extended eastward to meet it. In 1313 work was begun to extend the central tower. This was to trigger the need for the famous scissor arches to stabilise the structure. The two eastern transeptal chapels were finished in 1328 and 1329. All this was extremely expensive. Bishop John of Droxensford (1309–29) was the first to offer an indulgence for donations to the fabric fund. It is probable that his attempts to have William of March (1293–1302) canonised were a fund-raising enterprise. Droxensford had risen in the service of Edward I in his later years of grinding fund-raising. He seems to have been equally disliked by Edward II and the barons that opposed him. His lack of friends may help explain the dean and chapter being able to gain exclusive responsibility for running the cathedral (Colchester 1987 15–7).

POLITICAL CRISIS 1341–3

So Wells had a growing and an increasingly sophisticated and affluent citizenry. However, they lacked any rights of self-government. King John's charter had recognised them as free burgesses but it remained the bishop's borough. In such circumstances medieval townsfolk could still manage much. At Abingdon the Holy Cross Guild was to provide all of the almshouses in the churchyard, a rebuilt market cross, an enlarged church and a Thames bridge with an associated causeway. In Westminster the parish organisation was used instead.

A guild also appeared in Wells. It seems to have been a development from the Holy Trinity Guild in the parish church and St Cuthbert's was to provide its power base. In 1240 Bishop Joscelin had granted the advowson of the church to the dean and chapter. They kept the great tithes and installed a perpetual vicar. In 1262 Canon Richard de Bamfield gave a house opposite the church for a vicarage and it remains on that site. The guild came to supply other administrative support for the vicar. By the time records begin, it nominated churchwardens and administered the property and rents left to the Church mainly to secure obits. When one studies the town estate as it was in 1550 the original grants of 42 properties can be identified. Only 21 were left to the master and commonalty for their own purposes. Eight were left to the church, variously expressed as to St Cuthbert's, to the vicar, to the churchwardens or to the various guilds. One bequest of 1348 left two properties jointly to the town and churchwardens and 11 were left to the town for purposes connected with the church. Similarly, the annual rent of 4s from part of modern 57 High Street was originally granted to the vicar. In addition the guild began to penetrate the bishop's manorial structures, appointing jurors and verderers who made presentments. Verderies were the administrative subdivisions of the borough despite the rural-sounding name.

This status was not enough for some of the citizens. There survives an undated petition for a confirmation of John's charter which in fact asked for far more, including the right to appoint a mayor. Shaw suggests that this was probably submitted in 1307 soon after Edward II's accession (Shaw 1993 107-9). It was certainly unsuccessful. By the time the citizens tried again they faced a new bishop. Ralph of Shrewsbury became bishop in 1329. He was appointed at a time when the government was dominated by Edward II's widow, Isabella of France, and her lover, Roger Mortimer. Soon afterwards the young Edward III questioned the appointment and suggested an alternative. Ralph had to lobby Avignon to be sure of his position. Shortly after his delayed arrival he added the walls and moat to Joscelin's palace, probably in time for a visit from Edward III (Scrase and Dunning 2001). He took other actions to establish his position and order the diocese. For example in 1331 there were discussions of a scheme to house, and thus control, the vicars choral (HMC *Wells* i 219). Ralph was to push an alternative scheme through in 1348. In 1336 there was a hint that trouble was building. A group of citizens invaded the palace and attacked a group of strangers who were there with the dean.

In 1341 the citizens went behind the bishop's back and approached the king for a new charter granting them what they wanted, notably a mayor, courts and their own gaol. Edward was burdened by the costs of his French war. He was willing to oblige them to the sum of £40 without investigating the legal rights. The citizens appointed their first and only medieval mayor, Walter de Middleton, and bought further rights, notably a grant of murage for five marks. Murage was the right to levy tolls to finance a town wall.

Within three months questions were being asked in Chancery and the Exchequer about the legality of the charter. No doubt Ralph was behind the doubts. He was, of course, in the right. His borough was being stolen from him without compensation. Both he and the keeper of the county gaol at Somerton would suffer permanent losses. On 16 November 1341 the king issued a writ summonsing the citizens to explain why they should not lose their new charter. In the Michaelmas term 1342 the Court of Chancery quashed it.

Some burgesses would not accept defeat. They formed a sworn commune and, in effect, tried to continue the new regime despite the bishop and his officers. In January three of his officers were imprisoned. Over the next three months the bishops bailiff's attempts to hold hundred courts and view the frankpledge were disrupted. The dissidents refused to pay the bishop's customary dues. These were of two sorts. There was tolsester, the bishop's right to buy five flagons of any brewing of ale at a set low price. The second group were the tolls, dues and fines levied at the fairs. Not only did they refuse to pay but they began to collect what was due from outsiders backing their claims with bows and drawn swords.

Bishop Ralph now turned to the Courts in his own right. His initial action was against 29 men but the local jury added another 33, including Guy de Astington who was appearing as the citizens' attorney. These 62 have been studied in detail by comparing them with the property records and the details of the 1327 Lay Subsidy. To begin with, it is clear that the wealthiest citizens such as Thomas Testwode and Peter le Monier were not involved. More generally, 25 of those who paid in 1327 certainly survived until 1343. Only 12 were involved in the bishop's action. The most affluent had paid 8s, a further three 5s and five just 1s. Relative youth was also a factor. John le Ropere and Walter Compton were then at the start of careers which would make them major merchants, substantial landowners and masters of the guild. Family links were also significant. The alleged ringleaders, John le Kyng and Walter de Middleton, were at least stepbrothers. John's mother was Juliana la Kyng. Her second husband was Roger de Middleton and she outlasted him too. As she was still relatively young at the time of her remarriage they could have been half-brothers. More generally families acted together. All the Middletons and Eyrs were involved but no members of the substantial Churchstyle, Boghiare and de Mertoke families were. So the resistance can be characterised as led by the young, those representing the second level of wealth and their kin. But they also had popular support. Those named (particularly as the additional 33) include some 29 small traders who never featured as taxpayers, holders of property or became burgesses and members of the town guild (Scrase 2002a 39-40).

The bishop won and the named citizens were fined £3,000. This was probably kept as a threat held over their heads. Nevertheless, the ringleaders suffered. John le Kyng sold his Wells properties and left. Walter de Middleton stayed and was the only member of the group to be excommunicated. He fought back in a small way using the excuse of the Statute of Mortmain to stop paying a rent to the cathedral (in fact the Statute was not retrospective). He seems to have become very isolated. He was no longer asked to witness transactions. Then in 1355 he complained that the knight Richard de Acton and a group of locals had broken into his house, imprisoned him until he signed away his properties to Richard and left, carrying off his goods. Interestingly two of his attackers had been his associates in the commune, Guy de Astington and Nicholas Porter. If this was an attempt to run him out of town it failed. He was last recorded in 1358.

But for most life soon resumed its normal way. As we have seen, participation did not damage the careers of John le Ropere or Walter Compton. Indeed, the citizen body soon closed ranks. In April 1348 they had to deal with a bequest from Thomas le Devenysche. A bond was given by John le Ropere as master and 25 other burgesses. Of these 26, a total of 12 had been named in the bishop's action. Now they mingled with prominent non-joiners such as Testwode, le Monier and the Boghiere brothers. Indeed it is striking that for the leading citizens at the head of the list, names alternate. However, Walter de Middleton was not included (Scrase 2002a 40-1). The town guild needed consensus to function in the absence of legal powers. But it is also obvious that the bishop was willing to allow the guild to retain a role in manorial administration. The number of town-appointed officials steadily increased over the next 150 years. By the last quarter of the century, when town records first survive, the guild was not only appointing its master, rent collectors and the churchwardens but also two constables, two shambles wardens and four street wardens (the last being one for each verdery). The shared responsibility is shown in the way the shambles wardens reported offences in the market. Those committed by guild members were reported to the master and those by others to the bishop's bailiff. The guild was also selecting the two MPs although this did not preclude the bishop's officers or country landowners serving as well as burgesses. In 1384 the guild copied arrangements common in boroughs with legal powers of self-government. A council of 12 of 'the better men' was chosen to 'govern and rule the community'. Typically it was selected indirectly by a meeting of 50 burgesses (*CBI* 24).

DEMOGRAPHIC CRISIS BUT INCREASED PROSPERITY

The famine of 1315-19 had had an impact on Wells. While new development continued on Tucker Street (which had the stream and space needed by fullers) it is noticeable that vacancies were occurring in the more remote plots on the upper part of New Street by the 1330s. However, worse was to come. Plague arrived in 1348. Nationally it is reckoned to have carried off between a third and half the population. The impact cannot be quantified in Wells but many familiar names vanish after 1347 or 1348. Those who disappeared include Thomas Testwode and Peter le Monier. The heir to both was Margery Monier who probably became the richest lay person in medieval Wells. She did not remarry like the other wealthy Wells widows (that is Margery atte Churchstyle and Juliana la Kyng earlier in the century, or Isabel Tanner at the beginning of the fifteenth century) but seems to have made herself a unique place in the town. In 1363 she was a trustee of Walter Compton's will, a status gained by no other medieval Wells woman. An undated cathedral document probably from *c*.1380 concerns the lodging of a canon, William de Camera, who lacked a house. He was permitted to live in Margery's hired lodging which was presumably above suspicion.

13 Furniture in the Vicars' Hall. The vicars' communal building is remarkable for its medieval furnishing preserved in their original location. This is a bread bin from which the vicars would have taken their daily loaf of bread

Besides disrupting the elite the plague caused wider havoc. Of those listed in 1327 or 1343 some 42 were still alive in 1347–8 but only 13 can be traced after 1349. This must overstate the general death rate but the town certainly shrank. Plots with poorer access to the main business area fell vacant. New Street suffered and its east side was never to be built up so far northwards again. Independent properties vanished from Mede Lane and Monier Lane had more and more gaps.

Bishop Ralph retired to Wiveliscombe, his most remote manor, and remained there throughout the crisis. However, he did show his usual efficiency in arranging replacements for just under half of his clergy who died at their posts. He also pushed through his reform of the vicars' choral. These had formerly lodged about the town and their doings had frequently occasioned scandal. Now at the height of the outbreak the site of a canonical house was used to provide them with a new home. A hall was provided for communal eating and work started on the associated close where they were to live (*13* and *colour plates 13, 14* and *15*).

Vicars' Close is a remarkable survival of mid-fourteenth-century development. Interestingly, the oldest fragments of lay development are from about the same time. They form part of the bequest of Thomas le Devenysche, already referred to. He had acquired the sites of modern 36 and 38 High Street and late in his life redeveloped them, with five shops on the frontage with his hall behind. The three gables of the King's Head (*colour plate 27*) presumably represent three of the five bays of this structure, and relics of the hall can be seen in the inner rooms.

Although its population had dwindled and its physical extent contracted, Wells continued to prosper. Partly, this was a general phenomenon. As Alan Dyer has demonstrated, towns continued to thrive in the immediate aftermath of Black Death. This is linked to the resultant labour shortage. Surviving peasants did well and their standard of living improved. They were able to purchase more of the goods that towns provided (Dyer 1991). In addition there were particular factors behind this increased prosperity. The English cloth trade was beginning to boom and the northeast section of Somerset (extending north from Wells to Pensford and Bath and east to Frome) was at the heart of this expansion. The changes were partly technical as cloth was now fulled in mills rather than pounded by the feet of walkers in troughs. The streams running off the Mendips proved particularly suitable. In addition the disruptions of the Hundred Years War and Edward III's taxation policies meant that undyed broad cloth was now often exported instead of wool. Therefore these Somerset towns and surrounding villages such as Croscombe were at the forefront of change.

Rents of well-placed properties in Wells increased, compensating the institutional estates for losses at the periphery. Wealthy citizens also built up their own estates. Some 15 medieval burgesses can be shown to have owned over five properties. No less than five flourished for much of the period 1350 to 1400. Another two, Thomas le Saltare last documented in 1354 and Walter Compton who died in 1363, were active for part of the half century. The five were John le Ropere, Henry Boueditch, Richard Stowey, Nicholas Christesham and Thomas Tanner. Of these, Tanner is generally reckoned to have been the wealthiest merchant of medieval Wells but this may reflect the fact that we can discover more records of his activities than survive for earlier generations. As a group the five held the office of master for 20 years out of a documented 32 in this half century.

Tanner's property interests were large. He was to leave modern 29, 31, 33 and 42 High Street to support his chantry in St Cuthbert's. He also leased the dean and chapter's best property, the large so-called Compton's burgage. He had interests in number 74 and at least three other High Street properties. He owned 1 Market Place and 13 Sadler Street. There were also interests in a Southover property, one by St Andrew's Churchyard, and two in each of New Street and St Cuthbert's Street. He was also very active in the cloth trade. The aulnage accounts for 1395-7 record him as registering 424 'dozens' of cloths compared with 373 by Walter Dyer and 214 by Thomas Hore who both also served as master and a Wells MP or 41 by Thomas Jay another MP but never a master (17). Tanner seems to have spread the risk in his exports. The Bristol cloth customs for 1391-2 have six references to him but these involved only 64 cloths. One of the vessels he used from Bristol was the Wells owned *Marie*, whose existence is another testament to Wells importance in these years. But Tanner had his own ships for part of his career and must have used a variety of ports. In 1390 he was accused of evading customs on goods carried by his three ships operating variously from Redcliffe in Bristol, or Rooksmill or Crabhole on the river Axe (which may be another reason for his modest showing in the customs accounts). In one year he exported cloth and corn worth £640 to Spain and imported wine, nails and salt worth £359 6s 8d. Later, after his death, he was to be accused of trading with the enemy to the value of £200 but his widow Isobel was able to defeat the claim because of lack of detail (Carus-Wilson 1937 193-200; Dunning R.W. 1983 44).

This is a useful corrective to any tendency to think of the founders of chantries as necessarily exemplary individuals in life. Indeed Tanner was less tender to the souls of others. He failed to pay the obit rent due from 1 Market Place for four years and it was left to his widow to settle up paying £2 5s (Colchester 1988 45, 52, 60 & 68).

Tanner's career also demonstrates the point that the linkages of Wells were not limited to Bristol. As we have seen, Peter le Monier operated through Exeter and Dartmouth besides Bristol. Similarly, locational bynames demonstrate strong connections along the route first to Salisbury and then on to Southampton. Later property records and actions for debt show that the links to Salisbury continued after 1350. In addition, Wells fish dealers were buying produce at Exeter from 1370 (Kowaleski 1995 310-8). So a late fourteenth-century Wells merchant could have used any of Bridgwater, Bristol, Exeter, Southampton or the anchorages on the rivers of the Levels depending on source, urgency and bulk of cargo.

We can make a reasonable estimate of the population of this prosperous city for 1377 (*14*). In that year 901 persons paid the Poll Tax. Allowing for juveniles and the exempt poor this suggests a total of about 1,800 people. This makes Wells the most populous town in the county with Bridgwater next with 1,776 inhabitants. It was also sixth in the region. It is impossible to be clear whether its better performance than Bridgwater reflects some economic decline for the latter or merely shows that Wells had attractions for the less affluent. These would have included the possibility of much low paid work as servants, laundresses, grooms and the like around the cathedral and the frequent distributions of bread and alms associated with the commemorative services at both the cathedral and St Cuthbert's. Besides this lay population, a parallel clerical tax indicates 155 churchmen including school pupils and choristers.

1.t Bristol [3]	12,690	7. Bridgwater [46]	1,776
2. Salisbury [7]	6,746	8. Barnstaple [53]	1,576
3. Gloucester [18]	4,478	9. Cirencester [56]	1,492
4. Exeter [23]	3,332	10. Bath [69]	1,140
5. Plymouth [26]	3,098	11. Taunton [73]	1,078
6. **Wells** [44]	1,802		

14 Wells population in context for 1377

Numbers on left are regional rankings. Numbers in square brackets are national rankings after the *Cambridge Urban History of Britain I*, pp. 758–80.

Of the 1,800 lay inhabitants we can name only 124, a mere 7 per cent, and less than the 146 identifiable in 1327. The reason for this is changes occurring in the property market. Much property had been bequeathed to the institutional owners over the intervening fifty years. Once the vicars had their hall and close they too began to attract bequests. The first large benefaction was from a priest, John Hywysch, who left them several properties including 35 High Street which was to be their best rent. This leads on to the point that several cathedral clergy accumulated significant estates in Wells. Others were Walter de Hulle in the middle of the century and John Wareyn towards its end. The parts of John's estate in the city (as against East Wells) were left to endow a Wareyn Mass and part came to the vicars. Property also went to religious establishments elsewhere. In 1361 Sir Richard de Acton paid £10 for a mortmain license to alienate eight messuages, a shop, six tofts and eight acres of pasture in Wells and Barrow Gurney to the nunnery of Minchen Barrow. It is likely that this included the property extorted from Walter de Middleton, so Sir Richard may well have felt the need for prayers. It should also be remembered that simultaneously our five leading burgesses were accumulating estates, and that Margery Monier controlled Moniers Lane and at least 12 other tenements until she began to sell them from the 1360s. In addition, this period saw the first known estate accumulated by a layman who never joined the guild. He was a notary, Richard Horsforde, who mainly worked for the cathedral but also drew up many of the private property transactions of the time. Between 1363 and 1387 he acquired properties, particularly in New Street. As this was a marginal area, several were cottages and some tofts (vacant house plots) or gardens. As a result of these expanding private and institutional estates, property records (particularly abuttals) no longer give details of occupiers but just these owners. This is not fully compensated by the appearance of other records, notably the town authority's convocation books and the accounts of the cathedral communar and escheator (although as we shall see they do give other useful information).

The property records show the town assuming familiar attributes which were to last until about 1800. The first inns are recorded in the later part of the fourteenth century. Taverns are mentioned somewhat earlier. In 1358 Adam de Carleton was taken to the royal courts for building a cook shop in the middle of High Street (*15*). Part of his fellow burgesses complaint was that he was obstructing access to all of the taverns and butchers of the town. Initially these places were named for their proprietor. So we learn of Monier's Inn, Christesham's Inn and Adam de Cheleworth's Tavern. However, the first two were to survive and be renamed in a more familiar style. Monier's Inn became first the Bear and then the Angel while Christesham's Inn became the George. Again the original high cross was in place by around 1388.

To complete this chapter we must return briefly to events in the Liberty. Bishop Ralph of Shrewsbury lived on until 1363. He was responsible for one final reordering. In 1354 a house was built to accommodate the choristers and their master. A gable survives in the walled enclosure between St Andrew's Churchyard and the west cloister. By the time of his death Ralph seems to have been the subject of veneration, in contrast to the unpopularity of his early years. This may be connected to the fact that his last years were spent largely at Wiveliscombe, leaving day-to-day business to his suffragan. He was the hero of the *Historia Minor* as Ralph Ergum was to be of the *Historia Major*. Ralph of Shrewsbury's successor held the see for only three years. He, in turn, was succeeded by John Harewell who was bishop from 1366 to 1386. He was a considerable benefactor of the cathedral giving the bells named after him, a great west window and two-thirds

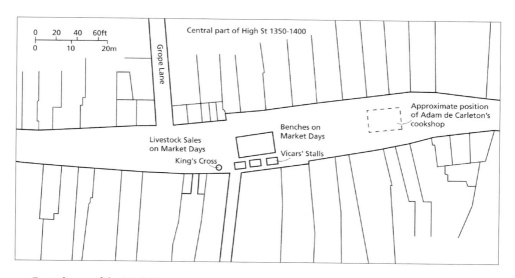

15 Central part of the High Street, 1350–1400

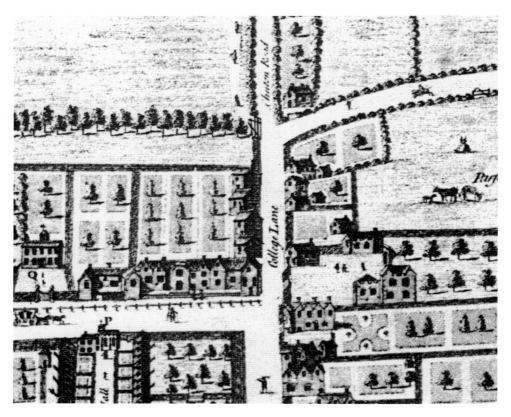

16 The buildings of the College of Montroy as shown by Simes in 1735 some 20 years before their demolition to make way for the Cedars

of the cost of the south-west tower. We know that the master mason William Wynford was responsible for the work on the tower. He had to solve the problems of relating the west front towers to the central tower and to the strong horizontal emphasis of the front. The next bishop had another short incumbency and was followed by Ralph Ergum, who held the see from 1388 to 1400. He addressed another problem of discipline. The vicars had been given a home but the priests who served the chantries and obits of the cathedral still lived where they could around the town. Early in his episcopate Ralph purchased Christesham's Inn from Nicholas Christesham and his wife Maud. He then vested it in the dean and chapter to manage on behalf of the chantry priests. Presumably this was a temporary home for them. By the time of his death he had provided funds to endow a college. Indeed preliminary work seems to have started in the last year of his life as the school which occupied the western half of the site was moved in 1399 (*9* and *16*). The next chapter will consider the college in more detail.

5

THE LATER MIDDLE AGES
1400–1523

The new century opened with little change. An older generation which had dominated the town was dying out. Thomas Tanner died in 1401 and Nicholas Christesham in 1404. But major cloth producers remained. Walter Dyer was active until 1427. In 1402-3 he was assessed on 127 broadcloths which, coming after his 373 'dozens' in 1395-7, shows that he was one of the county's leading producers (*17*). Nevertheless, the balance of power was probably shifting between the very affluent and the rest. Far more new names begin to appear as masters or MPs. Also in 1408 a new expanded council was selected. It was now to comprise of 12 of the greater (*majores*) and 12 of the middling (*mediocres*) burgesses (*CBI* 176).

One of Tanner's minor bequests was to Bishop Ergum's new college. This was to be referred to by a bewildering variety of names over the next 150 years. It could be the College of Montroy (from the location), of the Annuellari (as the priests performed annual commemoration services), New Hall (not to be confused with New Close which meant the vicars choral), of St Catharine or of St Anne. There were then various combinations such as St Anne in le Mountre (*16*). Once it could accommodate the priests the George Inn reverted to commercial use and became the college's best property. They also acquired

4–10 (evens) Sadler Street, and by a series of exchanges build up a holding in the triangle to the north of their house between New Street and what now became known as College Lane (modern College Street). In August 1410 the displaced school gave up its temporary home in Tor Street and moved to an outhouse on the north side of the entrance to 17 East Liberty just across the street from the college.

Vicars' Close was already evolving. It was originally designed as an elongated open quadrangle on to which the houses directly opened. The vicars soon demanded gardens and by around 1410 walled front gardens had been created reducing the public space to the present roadway.

The town was also confident enough to begin the construction of the great western tower of St Cuthbert's Church in about 1410. As this grew the church must have been truly striking as it also had a central tower.

Name	No. of cloths assessed for aulnage		No. of times post held		
	1395-7 in 'dozens' (duodene)	1402-3 broadcloth	Master	MP	Churchwarden
Thomas Tanner	424	– (dead)	6	2	–
Walter Dyer	373	127	3	1	–
Thomas Hore	214	65	4	1	–
Richard Groos	172	81	1	1	2
John Blithe	170	28	7	3	–
John Pedewell	71	47	1	1	–
John Newmaster★	51	2½	–	3	2
John Wycombe	51	2½	2	1	–
Richard Ferrour	48	11	–	1	–
Thomas Jay	41	– (still alive)	–	1	2
Roger Chapman	4	31	1	3	–
John Horewode	–	50	3	2	–
Thomas Wey	–	43 and 4 confiscated as contravening the standard	1	1	–

17 The elite, *c.*1400 and cloth production

★ discommoned (expelled) in 1410 and therefore no longer eligible for office

DIFFICULTIES BUT WITH OPPOSING TRENDS 1420–65

As explained, urban economies did well after Black Death. This could not last. After 1420 the pressures of wage inflation caught up with them. In Wells the most obvious sign was the collapse of the property market. The 1427/8 rental for the town estate shows both a large number of voids and a decline in rents of some 15 per cent. Thirty rents had fallen and only one concerned a rural parcel. The problems were greatest in High Street which should have been the most profitable area. There were 27 freehold properties here and no less than 17 had had their rents reduced. Even perpetual fixed rents might be effected. Thus the rent collectors could get only 1s from the tenement where Ilanta Phillipes had lived as it was derelict. It should have paid 10s. The cathedral escheator and communar had similar problems. Figure *18* shows fluctuations in the escheator's returns. From 1389 to 1410 he had been partly able to counter losses by increasing other rents. From 1410 there were no more increases but losses and reductions increased sharply. In the mid-1430s a more realistic escheator abandoned the pretext of various high rents which were always balanced by entries under losses. Subsequently, some rents were again raised but losses and reductions always outran them. Both the escheator and communar also had trouble with fixed rents. Some went unpaid for so long that the property could no longer be identified.

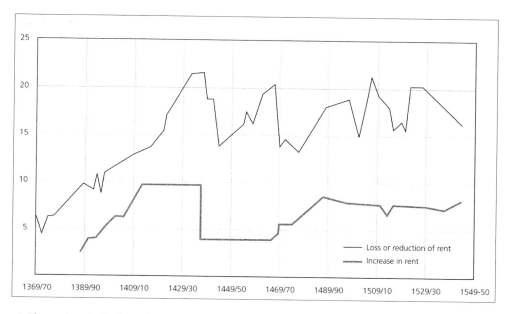

18 Fluctuations in Escheator's returns

Maintenance became a major problem and was not solved until the late sixteenth century. The key point was that it was a tenants' market. In the boom years it had been possible to pass the cost of repairs on to the tenant. Now if such provisions existed owners rarely thought themselves secure enough to enforce them. Sometimes they resumed responsibility for repairs. An opposite movement could only be achieved by a major rent reduction. The escheator tried this in Tor Street and his rents fell by 58 per cent. The town encouraged repair by temporary rent reductions or even, later in the century, by gifts of building materials.

It was even more difficult to obtain a tenant willing to build on a void site. It became common to waive fines and reduce rents until the building was complete. If the taker did not act there might be penalties in forfeiture of the lease, higher rents or a deferred fine. In 1446-7 the dean and chapter took a novel step. They rebuilt the larger Compton's burgage to create two new houses which they successfully let. This was to be a feature of their estate management thereafter and will be returned to below.

The other indicator of difficulties is the freeman admissions. Numbers for individual years vary widely. From the earliest record in 1377 to 1540 they range from a peak of 31 in 1467 to 14 separate years with no admissions. Behind the immediate variations there was a drop after 1420 and the 1450s were a particularly bad decade, with three years with no new freemen. In addition the composition of new burgesses changed. Fewer people from outside thought it worth paying a fine to join the guild. The proportion had been as high as 81 per cent in 1377-86. In 1457-66 it was down to 50 per cent. The other routes were by patrimony, marriage to a burgess' widow or to his daughter. Those using these methods paid less and were already committed to Wells in a way that strangers were not.

There were signs of dissension within the guild. In 1437 the town's customs were written down. Apparently, some of the 'laudable ordynances' had become 'somewhat withdrawn and negligently demised and not used'. A new council of 24 was appointed and the selection was made not by the elite but by four very ordinary members, none of whom ever rose higher than churchwarden (Serel 1875 36; Shaw 1993 171). Despite this episode the council had mixed fortunes. In 1467 only five members survived and it had to be refilled. This was a symptom of a lack of affluent persons to fill senior roles. It also explains why John Godwyn and William Vowell held between them sixteen terms as master in the period 1433 to 1466. There were insufficient alternative candidates.

An underlying reason for these difficulties may have been a decline in the cloth trade. Unfortunately, the aulnage accounts are not complete enough for us to be sure and the freeman lists show that the various textile trades were well represented. Tuckers are common and dyers, weavers and tailors all appear regularly. But it is clear that producers no longer dominated major offices in the town (*17*). This is apparent from 1416 and after John Pedewell's single term as master in 1422 nobody with that background served as master or MP until John Attwater's first term as master in 1458. In contrast, more gentlemen from outside and more bishop's officials served as MPs. When townsfolk were selected they were more varied. Hildebrand Elwell was a grocer, Henry Selwood a chapman, Thomas Langford a goldsmith and John Godwyn a glazier. Selwood was the only person to accumulate a private estate of over five tenements between the death of Isabel Tanner and the later career of John Attwater. Elwell is interesting as he left Wells for London, suggesting that the town was no longer adequate for the most ambitious.

However, these gloomy statistics are not the full story. Other events and records suggest a brighter side to the town's economy. To begin the building trades must have been buoyant largely thanks to two bishops. Bishop Nicholas Bubwith's impact was largely posthumous, coming from his bequests. He left money for a series of works around the cathedral and for an almshouse to serve the town. To begin, around the cathedral he provided funds for three schemes. First the cathedral's north-west tower was finally to be built thus completing the western facade. Next a library was to be provided over the whole length of the east cloister. The existing partial upper floor was removed and the southern section widened. This allowed the creation of the largest cathedral library in the country (*19*). Thirdly, he provided a chapel for Vicars' Close. This set the cathedral masons a problem as the site was small. For economy in both space and money the wall around the precinct was used for its rear. This meant that it was not square on to the Close. This is disguised by manipulating perspective. The observant will notice the signs of this. The roof ridge is not level but falls from east to west.

Bubwith's will of 1424 provided for an almshouse with 24 places. It was only in 1436 that an indenture was drawn up between the town guild and the dean and chapter. The town provided a site they owned north of St Cuthbert's while the dean and chapter paid for the building. The town was given a guildhall in the range and rights to nominate residents were shared. It proved an expensive project. This may explain why the north-west tower was a hollow shell with its inner surface of rubble or recycled stone and why no money was left for the roads and bridges of the county as the will provided.

The Statutes of the almshouse were drawn up in 1454 so it was operating by then. By that time it was accumulating its own estate. It and the College of Montroy suffered, as so much had been granted already. Also they were on peripheral sites while giving was always related to proximity. Nevertheless, the almshouse was given some 11 urban properties and rather more rural land. The town properties were often small and in less economically desirable areas, being in Beggar Street, Tucker Street beyond West Street, Tor Street, East Wells and the

19 The library as photographed by Phillips, *c.*1900. The view shows its length of over 48m (160ft). The anteroom is now used for exhibitions but the further parts are little changed. The shelving visible beyond is what was installed to replace losses during the Civil War and Commonwealth

upper part of New Street. The only High Street property was part of middle row. Its most substantial properties were in St Cuthbert Street comprising the two on the west of the vicarage and one by the churchyard.

The realisation of Bubwith's bequests took until after mid-century by which time the last great building bishop, Thomas Bekynton (*colour plate 9*), was at Wells. He was a native of Somerset and an early product of Winchester College. He then went into the royal household, acting first as tutor to the young Henry VI, subsequently as Secretary and finally as Keeper of the Privy Seal. He was about 60 when appointed to Wells so that the prospect might have been for a brief episcopate acting as a semi-retirement. The reality was very different. He held the see from 1443 to 1465. In his public career has had acquired an interest in building having been concerned with the construction of Eton College and Lincoln College, Oxford. He now displayed this interest not only in beautifying Wells itself but also at his other manor houses, notably his favourite, Banwell.

In the palace at Wells he provided a new more private domestic range on the north side of Joscelin's hall. This range was linked to the chapel by a cloister with

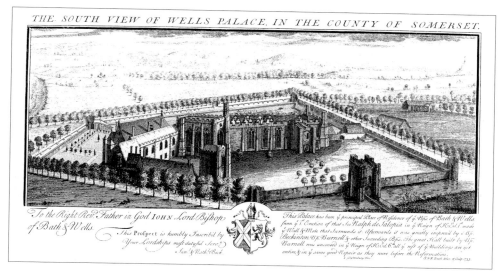

THE SOUTH VIEW OF WELLS PALACE, IN THE COUNTY OF SOMERSET.

20 The bishop's palace as drawn by the Buck brothers in 1733. It shows Bekynton's inner gate still in position (it had gone by 1735). Also compare with *colour plate 10* and front cover picture to see the appearance of the eastern range prior to its 'restoration' by Ferrey and the far more complete form of Burnell's great hall. *Courtesy Somerset Archaeological and Natural History Society*

an outer curtain wall. Set in this was an inner gate with a tower (*20*). This was the final medieval elaboration of the palace complex. The inner gate and cloister have vanished, as they were removed from 1640-1735 (*colour plate 18*).

His first major work to improve the town was the New Works begun in 1451. The main part of the scheme was a terrace of 12 houses built along the north side of Market Place, mainly on land taken from the churchyard but also with a strip from the road. The terrace was characterised by three-storey bay windows, one per house. Originally they had battlements as William Worcestre reported and as could still be seen in Simes' plan of 1735. Worcestre wrote that they cost above £500. Furthermore, the intention was larger. John Leland noted that, had Bekynton lived, a balancing terrace was intended on the south side of the street. A unified terrace was remarkable in fifteenth-century England. A unified square would have been unprecedented. The country did not get one until Inigo Jones' Covent Garden of the 1630s. The ambition of the scheme can be related to Bekynton's humanist circle which had strong Italian (and therefore Renaissance) links. One member of the group, Andrew Holes (Archdeacon of Wells 1450-70), had certainly visited Florence. The New Works probably represents an attempt to replicate efforts going on there to treat a square as a single artistic composition although here it was worked out in the Perpendicular Gothic style. As the south side was not built, an incumbent of the canonical house on Market Place was

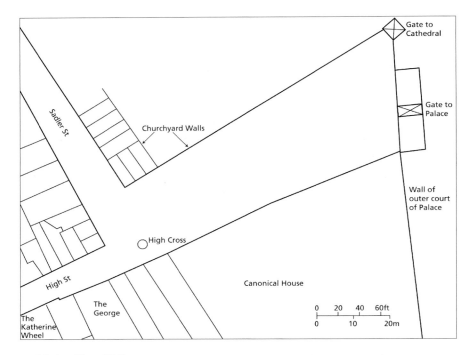

21 Market Place, Wells, *c.* 1400

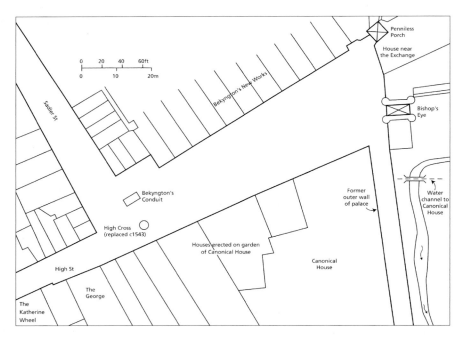

22 Market Place, Wells, *c.* 1500

inspired to develop his side garden with a range of three properties in vernacular style. The largest soon became the Crown Inn (*21* and *22, colour plates 18* and *19*).

The residential scheme also included three more modest houses on the east of Sadler Street. They also straddled the precinct wall and replaced the bishop's guildhall. The scheme had other implications. Originally the New Works lacked adjoining gardens, although strips were later rented from the dean and chapter. Instead gardens were provided on a piece of the bishop's land south of the millstream and on the north edge of the coneygree. This raised questions of access. A new roadway was provided along the eastern boundary of the canonical house. This involved setting back the outer wall around the palace, which in turn involved alterations to the gates. This was done in a grand manner. The gate towards the palace was, in Bishop Ralph of Shrewsbury's time, described as a gateway with a hall and chambers on both sides all under one roof. Now the gates were provided with embattled towers. Worcestre tells us that the Bishop's Eye alone cost over 200 marks (£133.33). A third gate, Brown's Gate was provided adjoining the Sadler Street terrace. This group of houses and gate cost another 200 marks.

Penniless Porch, the gate from Market Place to the cathedral, was changed in another way. The former gate had a straight passage and visitors had approached the cathedral via a door in the west cloister. The cathedral archaeologist, Dr Warwick Rodwell, has recently had this highlighted in paint. The building of the choristers' house made this less appropriate. Bekynton had the wall built which screens the house and the area where the choristers could play from the churchyard. In what must be related as a single scheme, Penniless Porch now turned through a right angle directing visitors to the west front or the present door into the cloisters.

The development also drew attention to water supplies. A pipe ran under the New Works feeding a dipping well in each. Also in 1451 the bishop made an agreement with the townsfolk to improve their supply. This was granted in perpetuity from the great well and the bishop provided both the conduit house by the spring and the grand outlet in Market Place. The guild was responsible for the lead pipes. A final water scheme was agreed in 1464. Richard Swan who held the Market Place canonical house was granted a supply. In return he was made responsible for what had been the outer wall of the palace but had been cut off by the new road although it still served as his eastern boundary.

The bishop built one more gate, started in 1459, when the dean and chapter agreed to his proposal. It was the Chain Gate which provided the vicars with a sheltered route from their hall to the cathedral (*colour plate 5*). It could also be portrayed as a further stage in the process of segregating them from the temptations of the wider world. Another scheme was only implemented after his death. This was to provide an upper floor to the west cloister. The accommodation was to provide a practice room for the choristers, an audit office and a new site for the school. His executors were able to carry out one other operation. Any residual of his estate was to be used 'for some charitable purpose, such as the repair of roads and bridges or the relief of the poor'. His trustees actually used the money to provide better chimneys for the houses of Vicars' Close, giving the properties what remains one of their most striking features. As with Bubwith's will, the Somerset roads were the losers.

So Bekynton beautified the town, kept the building trades busy and gave the cathedral a new vigorous intellectual life. However, one must ask: what were his intentions? His modern biographer thought that the housing was intended to finance his chantry. But more was involved. The property rents far exceeded the chantry's costs. This income was obviously intended to help the dean and chapter's finances. Indeed, it was significant that the income went to the communar who controlled general finances rather than the escheator who was responsible for memorial services. In addition it should be apparent that the housing cannot be considered alone. It was physically and conceptually linked to other elements. Probably, the key motive was to move his flock to deeper devotion by flamboyant display which embraced both grand settings and splendid liturgies as at Eton. In this context it is worth noting that he provided new and, for the period, remarkably humane regulations for the choristers. Certainly, Bekynton intended to beautify Wells. Partly it may have been intended to act as his memorial and it may also have been meant to demonstrate new approaches to design. But above all it reflects his passion for building schemes, which he saw as a means of moving the seers to greater faith.

The New Works are significant in other ways. They finally carried the built-up area up to the cathedral. They also demonstrated that good quality properties at some of the highest rents in town could be let. Obviously part of the population was affluent although landlords struggled to find tenants elsewhere. The New Works thus finished the migration of the town's best properties towards the cathedral. In 1327 many of the richest citizens lived at the west end of High Street or in St Cuthbert Street. From this time they tend to be found along the western boundary of the Liberty.

The town also contributed to the building boom by continued improvements to the parish church. The west tower was completed about 1430 but it was followed by a long series of works to recast the structure in Perpendicular form. Nor was the interior neglected. Here the major work was rather later. In 1470 the guild commissioned a Jesse Tree to balance Tanner's chantry in the opposite transept.

Another sign of prosperity was the continued presence of foreign persons. In 1449 they were the subjects of a poll tax. Wells had three Germans, two

Dutchmen, a Frenchman and six foreign servants. In Somerset only Taunton had a comparable number. Furthermore, it was still worthwhile for foreigners to remain and make a commitment to the town. In 1468 and 1471 Dutchmen were admitted to the freedom.

There were also signs of continued enterprise by the citizens. They were obviously exploring the potential of the Dorset ports. Hildebrand Elwell had interests in Bridport and Henry Selwood sat as MP for Lyme in 1442. Selwood's contacts were wide as he also dealt with London grocers. It could also be that there was still involvement with the cloth trade, but that the participants no longer held high office in Wells. From the Wells records Roger Martyn seems obscure. He became a freeman in 1438 but never held any important office, or played a significant part in the property market. However, the Southampton Brokerage Book for 1439–40 reveals him as an important merchant. In that period only 2 per cent of over 1,600 wagon trips from Southampton (plus three packhorses bound for Bath) went to Somerset. Frome took 14 full and a part load, Bruton seven loads, Wells five and Taunton four. The Frome trade was mainly controlled by a Southampton merchant and only he routed direct. Other loads changed carts, usually at Salisbury. The Taunton loads were for at least three different men. In contrast Roger Martyn and Thomas Ede of Bruton took all their town's loads. Martyn had four deliveries via Salisbury and one via Warminster. His final load was all of wine. The others had together the following part-loads, three of madder, two of woad, one of iron, one small consignment of wine for personal use and a larger amount of wine. He was either involved in, or was supplying the cloth trade, as the presence of the dyes madder and woad show.

All this seems to show a decline in population and perhaps less willingness to be involved in town affairs. Nevertheless, Wells still contained persons of enterprise and affluence.

THE YEARS OF THE ABSENTEE BISHOPS 1466–1523

Bishops had often been great officers of state. As a result they had been absent from their diocese. However, when they did come to Somerset they drew extra visitors. Now for a period of over 50 years the county rarely saw its bishop. Some never came to their diocese. Bekynton's successor was Robert Stillington who had been Edward IV's chaplain. His episcopate ran from 1466 to 1491 but he spent only three and-a-half weeks in the diocese. Certainly, he was for a time a minister of state. But the main reason was another darker matter. If Edward indeed had a precontract with Eleanor Butler (which would have invalidated his marriage to Elizabeth Woodville) then Stillington was involved. Thus Edward,

Richard III and Henry VII all had strong reasons to keep him close at hand even when he was not imprisoned. He managed only one visit to Wells. While there he did order a grand rebuilding of the Lady chapel in the Cloister. It was to be in the Perpendicular style and aligned with the rest of the cathedral. He never saw it completed (*6, colour plates 3* and *8*).

In his absence the town's fortunes improved. Partly, it must have been what economists now call multiplier effects from Bekynton's expenditure. The cloth trade also revived although it was organised differently. In the late fourteenth and early fifteenth centuries there had been a large number of producers. Now the trade was dominated by a single clothier. This situation was to continue until the mid-sixteenth century. Until 1500 the dominant figure was John Attwater. He was succeeded by John Mawdeley.

The improved prospects were reflected in an increase in guild membership. This ran on from 1467 with 31 admissions to 1478 with 22. Partly, this may reflect a deliberate campaign. Certainly, the rules were changed to permit former apprentices to be admitted at the lower rate charge for entry by patrimony or marriage. But even so entrants must have perceived advantages in joining. In 1467 no less than 18 were outsiders willing to pay the full fine. The composition of the entrants is interesting. Eight were involved in textile trades. Another seven were in appropriate urban crafts, bakers, a saddler, a carpenter and the like. However, three were bishop's officers and one the cathedral sacristan. This was unprecedented.

The reason was not a charm offensive by the bishop. He was at Court involved in Edward's schemes to reduce the Nevilles' power. It was certainly linked to the selection of the William Edmund, described as 'of Reading and Wells, gentleman', the bishop's bailiff and Thomas Smyth, the bishop's apparitor, as the MPs for that year (although Edmund had already served in 1447 and 1449-50). It may be that long-serving officials felt lost without a resident bishop. Certainly, it resulted in a unique period of integrated government. Edmund and Smyth served as constables that year under the master John Attwater. They became members of the council but never masters. The guild gained by this. In 1473 the master, acting in the guild's court, forced Smyth to withdraw fines he had imposed on three burgesses while carrying out the bishop's jurisdiction. This may explain why the experiment was not repeated.

At just this time the nature of the guild's annual appointments began to change. In the earliest records they comprised a master, two of each of the constables, rent collectors, churchwardens and shambles wardens plus four street wardens. Between 1400 and 1472 two more two-man posts had been created. They were custodians of the altars of the Blessed Mary and the Holy Trinity. The latter were alternatively described as the guardians of the Holy Trinity

Guild. In 1473 a town clerk was added. Then over the next 30 years a further six two-man posts appeared. Only the conduit wardens involved a municipal duty. The other posts involved further altars comprising those of Jesus, St Katherine, St Anne, St Erasmus and Holy Cross. This certainly widened public involvement. Indeed, participation went beyond guild membership. This was partly to allow Out Parish involvement in the religious duties but also the demand for street wardens was such that others had to be involved. This was particularly common in working-class Southover which had fewer members. By the 1520s the effort had proved too much. The churchwardens also acted as custodians of the altar of St Erasmus and appointments had been abandoned to St Katherine's altar. Nevertheless, the exercise gave more people some status in town affairs.

After 1478 the economy again experienced difficulties. Freemen numbers declined. In 1482 and 1486 nobody was admitted. In the three decades from 1487 to 1516 only 36 per cent of entrants paid the full fines. The problems of vacant properties and repairs had never been solved and now they worsened.

From 1486 to 1513 there was a new focus of power in Wells. He was Thomas Cornish, titular Bishop of Tenos. This was an Aegean island with an Orthodox population and, by this time, Turkish rulers. Western Christendom retained the title as one of the relics of the Fourth Crusade. In fact the title gave him status and he acted as suffragan of Wells. The absentees still enjoyed the bishop's income so other arrangements had to be made to support him. He was (to list only the most important) a canon residentiary, successively Provost and Precentor of the cathedral, prior of the Wells hospital, vicar of both St Cuthbert's and Chew Magna and Provost of Oriel College, Oxford. There had been suffragans before, but Cornish's position was strengthened by the almost complete absence of a resident bishop and a long period at Wells. He built up a group of kinsmen and other associates around him.

He seems to have kept up the intellectual life of the cathedral. Certainly, we have Polydor Vergil's appreciation early in the new century. In his *Anglica Historia* he refers to the chapter as 'a famous college of priests, men of honest behaviour and well learned'. Music was also reaching a peak, with two successive masters of the choristers and two successive succentors of national significance. The earlier appointed, Richard Hygons and Henry Abyndon were in post when Cornish arrived. But he must have played a part in securing successors of status, Richard Bramston *alias* Smith and Robert Wydowe.

Cornish began to build up a property holding with particular emphasis on inns. The earlier name of the Cornish Chough for what became the Mitre on Sadler Street suggests a link. He certainly controlled the Star (*colour plate 26*) and Antelope while his nephew, John Welshote, held the lease of the Katherine Wheel. Cornish rebuilt the Antelope having been granted an 80-year lease by the dean and chapter in 1501. Another of his associates, Walter Strowde, was installed in it. There are a number of different aspects to the Antelope development. Firstly, it was an aid to the cathedral's finances. The dean and chapter had continued to redevelop to improve returns. In 1497 a Sadler Street property was removed and replaced. The larger unit became an inn, the Hart's Head (later the White Hart). It was adjoined by a smaller property, demolished in modern times. But money was short for investment. Cornish's scheme gave them a redevelopment at no cost. It was their preferred method from that date. In 1509 and 1515 another canon, Peter Carslighe, was granted similar 80-year leases on first 14 and then 15 New Street. The former had been let at a reduced rent since 1432 and the second had been a vacant site since a fire between 1403 and 1408. There was also a traditional motive. Cornish, the succentor Thomas Lugwardyn who had contributed funds and Bishop King were to receive obits for 99 years. Also Cornish seems to have been interested in building. He rebuilt his canonical house (the modern museum) while Chew Magna Church has windows carrying his initials.

Bishop Fox had a short episcopate (1492-4) before moving on to Durham. He was a busy royal servant and never visited his diocese. Nevertheless, he did find time to look at his rights. In 1493 the guild was startled to receive a series of probing questions from him as follows:

1. why did they hold themselves the king's burgesses rather than his?
2. why did they claim the power to make burgesses?
3. why did they refuse to accept burgesses made by his bailiff but submitted them to their own processes? and
4. why had they opened strange mills when manorial custom bound them to his?

They sent their initial answers to Fox at Kenilworth. He was not satisfied and threatened to go to law. A further deputation found him at Warwick. After considering the evidence submitted, which included both the city charters and bishops' custumals, the bishop abandoned the matter but he obviously found the citizens too self-assertive bidding them 'sette aparte all wilfulnesse and haultesse'. They must be content to live under the right of the Church (CBII 180).

Bishop King was also busy in the king's service. Before he came to Wells the town had witnessed the eastward march of the Cornish rebels. King arrived the day before Henry VII, no doubt to arrange his reception. The palace must have been suffering from 30 years of neglect, so Henry was accommodated in the newly rebuilt deanery. Henry either believed that Wells and Somerset had been friendly to the rebels or purported to do so as a means of raising money from a rich county. The county had to pay £7,677 13s 4d and Wells £313 13s 4d of this (for comparison, Taunton had to raise over £400).

The money was collected in 1499 and 1500. The records provide a useful survey of the more affluent. Sums paid range from £1 to £40 and, besides citizens, three cathedral officers and a widow paid. The profile is very similar to 1327. The top 13 paid 61.5 per cent of the whole and the top third 76 per cent. The hierarchy of wealth fits with what is known from other records except for the two top payments which were each of £40. One of the payers was John Tyler. He was master in these years and would have been expected to make a disproportionate contribution. The other was a Southover tanner, John Smith. He was a member of the elite but there is no indication of great wealth. The great Wells fortunes had all been linked to wool and cloth. So there may be an element of exemplary punishment indicating that he had supported the rebels.

Otherwise, the list looks like a levy according to wealth. The four who paid the next highest sum of £13 6s 8d comprises of the two clothiers Attwater and Mawdeley, together with Richard Burnell and John Usthwayte. Of the 11 who paid £10 or more, if we disregard the widow and a cleric as ineligible, all but three served as master on several occasions. Together they totalled 23 terms up to 1500 and a further 13 afterwards. Of the others, Robert Draper might have served if he had outlived his father by longer. Again, the widow was Margaret Vowell whose husband Richard was master four times. In contrast, only two of those paying lesser sums were to become master in the following two decades. The number of elite was small and several members were old. The recovery from 1467 was over.

It is from this time that we get the first indications of what are usually seen as typical medieval institutions, but in Wells are not fully documented until the period 1550 to 1610. The first of these concerns the ceremonial life of the town. In 1497 the town records make no reference to the passage of the Cornish rebels. But they do report an enquiry as to what had become of the proceeds from the Robin Hood ceremony. The second relates to the existence of trade companies. They are not fully identified until 1555. At that time one was the Tailors Company, and it alone of the companies had some property. The benefactor was John Orchard, who bequeathed it for the use of the poor tailors of Wells. Now he flourished at this time rising to be churchwarden in 1494 and 1495. As he did not contribute towards the fine he was probably dead before 1499. So the Tailors Company must have been in existence before that time.

The limited elite led to guild conflict in 1510-2. Nobody was willing to undertake the role of rent collector. Master Nicholas Trappe nominated John Welshote who rejected the suggestion in such insulting terms that he should have been discommoned (expelled from the guild). This did not occur but it took a year to achieve reconciliation. Welshote may have been handled with care as the nephew of Bishop Cornish. Indeed, at one stage he threatened to refer the dispute to the king and council using his uncle's influence. Convocation Book contrasts his outbursts, with Trappe shown as reasonable, patient and anxious to conciliate. This portrayal as a model master reflects a tendency of late medieval town records to set out an official view of what should have happened. This trend was intensified by the employment of a professional clerk. The clerk, John Beynton, had shortly before contrasted the loyalty of Wells in 1497 with that of Taunton. This was despite the fact that he had paid £1 towards the fine.

Bishop King's two successors, Hadrian de Castello and Cardinal Wolsey, never came near their diocese. However, Hadrian did send a personal representative from Italy in the form of his nephew, the historian Polydor Vergil. Vergil was made Archdeacon of Wells and installed in the canonical house which is now the music school. He retained the post through the religious reforms of Henry VIII and Edward VI. But he spent much time in London and periodically returned to Italy. His tenure was marked by periodic difficulties with the government. Already in 1515 he spent a period in the Tower when an intercepted letter revealed indiscreet comments on Wolsey's ambition.

After 1500 economic problems intensified. The property market declined further. Newly acquired properties help support income but vacancies and difficulties with repair intensified. It had long been necessary for cathedral staff to contribute to make up the escheator's deficit in bad years. In good years a refund was made from the surplus. The last distribution was in 1502-3. Thereafter a subsidy was always necessary. Similarly, in 1511 the town made incoming councillors contribute towards the rebuilding of a decayed High Street property.

Burgess numbers also tumbled. In the first two decades of the new century they must have been lower than at any time since 1377. Nobody was admitted in any of the years 1508, 1511, 1515 and 1517. This may explain a change in the system of honours. Previously, it had been very rare for masters to have previously served as churchwarden. Instead that post served as the culmination of the career of the 'middling sort'. From about 1515 those proceeding to their first appointment as master had with one exception served as churchwarden (although the earlier role continued). This seems to have been a way to encourage the affluent to join by rapid recognition. For example, William Sabyne was admitted in 1518 and became churchwarden that year.

So the town economy was in a bad state when the general economy began to decline. This recession related to three elements. Firstly, 1518-9 were bad years for epidemics, possibly including a virulent influenza. Secondly, there were a series of bad harvests, beginning in 1519 when it was said to have rained from May to Christmas. Poor yields continued for a further two years and distress spread through Europe. At this inappropriate time the Emperor Charles V launched an aggressive foreign policy. His preparations and Francis I of France's response soaked up capital. Demand for English cloth fell both at home and abroad.

In this poor state Wells had to face two pressures. To begin there was a greater bishop's presence, although the transition was gradual. Bishop Clerk had been Wolsey's chaplain and was employed by him on diplomatic missions. Secondly, there was a far-reaching tax to allow Henry VIII to join his peers in the royal sport of war.

Above: 1 Wells from the south showing the landscape setting. The viewpoint is from the farm access bridge over the southern relief road. This view shows clearly how the city is constrained by the Bishop's Park in the foreground and the Mendips in the background. Note the dramatic impact of the cathedral while most of the town is lost amongst the trees

Right: 2 This air view of the town from the west shows clearly that the cathedral and most of the bishop's palace are set at a different angle to the roads and buildings of the rest of the town. *Courtesy Professor Mick Aston*

Above: 3 The 1978-9 excavations in the Church Camery revealing the foundations of Stillington's Lady Chapel and beneath them an earlier set of buildings on a substantially different alignment which is actually that of the town. *Courtesy Dr Warwick Rodwell*

Left: 4 St Andrew's Spring. This forms the end of the early alignment running from Market Place through the Anglo-Saxon cathedral and St Mary's Chapel (6). The niche in the medieval wall enabled pilgrims to kneel and pray while looking at the holy well. It should be noted that many (including the Ordnance Survey) have wrongly called the main group of springs (shown in *colour plate 7*) St Andrew's Well

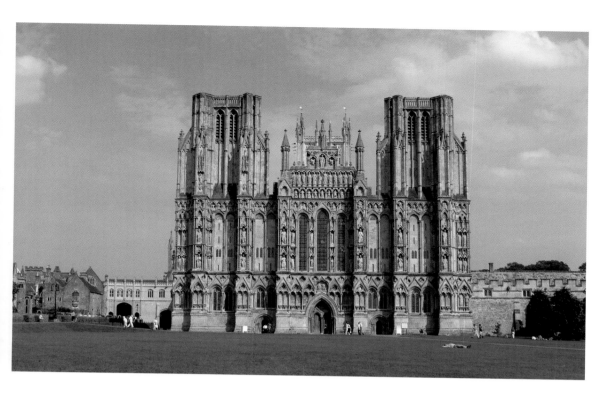

Above: 5 The west front of the cathedral with the west cloister to the right and Bekynton's Chain Gate on the left. This impressive group differs from its medieval appearance in two ways. First, and most important, the nearly 300 medieval statues that adorn the front were painted. Second, the cloister wall was rendered so that it resembled the ashlar of the cathedral. *Courtesy Faculty of the Built Environment, UWE*

Right: 6 The cathedral foundation raft exposed by the west front prior to repaving. The holes were made to support scaffolding. The foundations comprised 1.4m (4ft 3ins) of stone in mortar. The form of the foundations here confirms that the deeply embayed form of this facade was a late change of plan. Above the foundations fragments of paint were found, representing drips and spills when the statues were painted. *Courtesy Historic Environment Group, Somerset County Council*

Left: 7 The cathedral from the east looking across the main springs to the central tower, quire and Lady Chapel. The exact form of the springs has varied sharply over time reflecting the use of sluices to divert flow to the moat, mills and water supplies, and, in recent times, garden design. St Andrew's Well is beyond the trees and shrubbery that partially hid the Lady Chapel

Below: 8 The Church Camery soon after Rodwell's excavation. The ground plan of Stillington's Chapel is clear. Something of its interior decoration survives on the east cloister around its former door. Elsewhere the cloister wall shows the contrast between the rubble of the original single storey and the ashlar used for the library. *Courtesy Historic Environment Group, Somerset County Council*

Right: 9 Bishop Bekynton from the effigy on his tomb. As the tomb was made in his lifetime it is probably a fair likeness. It is also the best survival to show us how the painted statuary must have looked in the Middle Ages. *Courtesy the Chapter of Wells Cathedral*

Below: 10 The bishop's palace today. From right to left the elements are the remains of Bishop Burnell's hall, the chapel, Bishop Joscelin's original range and Bishop Bekynton's domestic quarters. Contrast with *20* to see the changes since 1734. The inner gate tower has gone, Burnell's great hall has been reduced to two walls and the facade of Joscelin's hall was remodelled by Ferrey, *c.*1850

Left: 11 The view from the south-east turret of the palace walls looking up the moat. The flow from the springs can be seen at the head of this reach. Beyond the town is at its narrowest north to south and nearly vanishes into the wider landscape

Below: 12 The space between the palace moat and the south cloister. Today this is a tranquil spot embellished by Victorian tree planting. It was very different in earlier periods. It then featured the so-called Cow House, the bishop's prison for offending clergy, together with a pond where wagoners and market traders watered their horses

13 View from the cathedral tower showing Vicars' Close prior to its repaving. Beyond and to the left are St Andrew's Lodge and the canonical house at 11 North Liberty. Top right can be seen some of the cedars which gave the Tudway mansion its name. Subsequently, they were depleted by storm damage. *Courtesy Historic Environment Group, Somerset County Council*

14 23 Vicars' Close showing medieval painted wall plaster revealed during works. *Courtesy Historic Environment Group, Somerset County Council*

Left: 15 The chapel at Vicars' Close. The chapel occupies the ground floor while the vicars' library was housed above. The fall in the line of the roof ridge can be clearly seen. Note also the impact of the repaving replacing the former asphalt. *Courtesy Faculty of the Built Environment, UWE*

Below: 16 St Cuthbert's Church. The parish church does not get the attention it deserves due to the proximity of the cathedral. In fact, it is an excellent building with one of the best west towers in Somerset. It would have been even more remarkable prior to the collapse of the central tower. It is a testament to the prosperity of the medieval townsfolk

Above: 17 The fifteenth-century Bishop's Barn. The area to its north, now a children's playground, was once the Coneygree where rabbits were kept for the bishop's table

Right: 18 Market Place looking east in 1991. Compare the Bishop's Eye and adjoining properties with their form in *36, 46* and *48* to see that their historic air conceals considerable change. Also contrast with the next picture to see the impact of repaving and removal of double yellow lines

Above: 19 Market Place looking west in 2001 with the town hall on the left. This view shows the effect of the recent repaving. Note also the twentieth–century changes to the town hall in contrast to *39. Courtesy Faculty of the Built Environment UWE*

Left: 20 Charles Tudway as portrayed by Gainsborough. Understandably he looks well pleased with his improved fortunes. The background landscape cannot be certainly identified as is the case with many Gainsborough portraits. *Courtesy Courtauld Institute of Art*

Opposite above: 21 The Cedars, 15 North Liberty, the mansion that Charles Tudway had built. The portion on the left is the conservatory added by John Paine Tudway. The whole is now part of Wells Cathedral School

Opposite below: 22 19 East Liberty. The house Claver Morris built at a cost of £807 14s 6¾d. Note the old-fashioned mullioned windows on the flank compared with the sash windows on the front. The flat over the porch was a favoured vantage point for the doctor. From here he watched scenes as varied as a hanging at Keward (aided by his new telescope) and an eclipse

Left: 23 The old archdeacon's house during its 'restoration' by Buckle after use as Assembly Rooms and a brewery and prior to its occupation by the theological college. This watercolour by A.A.Clarke captures the form of the medieval hall stripped of later additions. The hall was built by Andrew Holes and was later occupied by Polydor Vergil. *Courtesy the Chapter of Wells Cathedral*

Below: 24 The modern museum, 8 Cathedral Green and beyond the crenellated walls and gatehouse of the Old Deanery. The museum was one of the bishop's canonical houses. Despite later changes, notably the insertion of Georgian windows, elements of the house built by Bishop Cornish are still apparent

Above left: 26 The Star, High Street. The building is no longer an inn after over 450 years. It was first documented in 1513 when it was one of Bishop Cornish's holdings. In 1606 it was described as an ancient inn. The present facade is of the eighteenth century

Above right: 25 The Swan, Sadler Street. This is the oldest surviving inn in Wells, having carried this name and been on this site since 1422. Its form reflects rebuilds of 1549 and 1768. It was the corporation's best rent until Clement Tudway bought it in 1800

Right: 27 The King's Head, High Street (the property where the building line moves forward). The brick front hides a much earlier structure hinted at by the gabled roof and revealed in the interior. It was converted to an inn in 1605. Its name relates both the accession of James I after half a century of ruling queens and the fact that John King leased the site from the corporation. The break in the building line reflects the fact that the property is just to the west of the former middle row

Above: 28 The Sherston Inn, Priory Road. Another long-running inn having occupied this site since at least 1589. But in contrast to the Swan it has had many names being successively the Black Bull, White Horse, Sherston Arms, Railway Hotel and Sherston. Also it faced Southover until the making of Priory Road. The principal facade with its parapet wall reflect the rebuild of 1862, intended to take advantage of the arrival of the railways. The roundabout beyond is on the site of the former level crossing

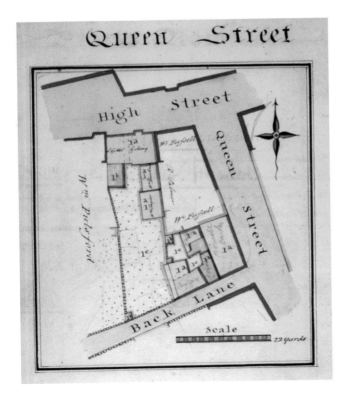

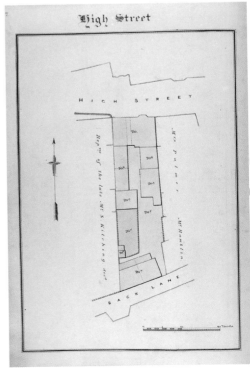

Above: 31 The same area as shown in the previous two plates today. The nineteenth-century encroachment is clearly seen. Beyond is the City Arms. The prison was in the nearer range which has the rounded end created by the 1821 road improvement

Right: 32 Detail from St Thomas Street. Because of its working-class nature this area had a tradition of adapting properties rather than rebuilding. As a result relics of early forms can be found either in use as with this door or as fragments of tracery visible in the walls

Opposite below, left: 29 Corporation properties in Queen Street and the west end of High Street from the 1821 survey. The survey represents a high point of the cartographers' art. Compare the High Street property and the road in front of it with the next picture

Opposite below, right: 30 Modern 73 and 75 High Street from the Corporation survey of 1848. In contrast to the last, the property has gone from two frontage properties with two behind to two on both the High Street and Market Street frontages with five in a court between. Also, note how the property to the west has fenced off part of the road while 80 opposite has built forward at the expense of public space

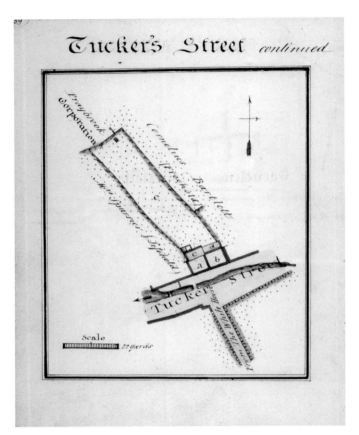

Tucker's Street continued

Left: 33 Tucker Street from the 1821 survey. This pair of houses and a further 14 to their west were removed to make way for the railway line from Yatton and Cheddar and the associated goods yard. A further eight were lost on the south. The property to the east is now the Cheddar Valley Inn. Note also the open stream in the street which was the last unculverted portion of the Ludbourne

Below: 34 Tucker Street today with the Cheddar Valley Inn as the westernmost property on the north side. The inn's name derives from the popular name of the western railway approach to Wells. Note how the spire of St Cuthbert's dominates this side of the town

6

THE END OF THE MEDIEVAL SYSTEM: REFORMATION, ECONOMIC DECLINE AND SELF-GOVERNMENT 1524-1603

The tax that Wolsey had developed for Henry VIII was a radical change. Previous lay subsidies had been on movables (that is goods). This was on the best of movables, wages or rent from land. Anybody possessing more than £1 in any of these would pay. Furthermore, it was to be levied in each in 1524 and 1525. The number caught expanded vastly. In 1327 there were 64 payers and now, with a lower town population, there were 221. We thus have a picture of Wells at the end of the Middle Ages. It should be remembered that it was a picture of a town in recession. In 1521 and 1524 no freemen were admitted. In the latter year the escheator's accounts had their longest list ever of losses and reductions in rent while the balancing list of increases vanished.

To begin with the general context, Wells despite its economic difficulties had improved its position both nationally and in the region. In 1334 it stood at eighty-sixth nationally and twelfth regionally in terms of wealth. Now it was sixtieth nationally and ninth in the south-west. In terms of payers it was seventy-fourth overall and again ninth in the region (23). Furthermore, this has to be read in the light of Alan Dyer's comment that 'Gloucestershire and Somerset clearly escaped the searching assessment of the other counties' (Dyer 2000 761-7). It remained the second town in the county but now Taunton was ahead of it while Bridgwater's economy had collapsed.

Ranked by assessed wealth (one year's maximum payment)		Ranked by number of taxpayers	
1. Bristol [3]	£479	1. Bristol [3]	1,166
2. Exeter [6]	£441	2. Exeter [6]	1,050
3. Salisbury [7]	£411	3. Salisbury [8]	885
4. Gloucester [19]	£134	4. Gloucester [27]	466
5. Taunton [40]	£86	5. Plymouth [44]	310
6. Plymouth [44]	£85	6. Taunton [49]	300
7. Ottery St Mary [46]	£79	7. Ottery St Mary [62]	250
8. Dorchester [47]	£77	8. Cullompton [64]	245
9. **Wells** [60]	£61	9. **Wells** [74]	221
10. Cullompton [61]	£60	10. Shaftesbury [77]	213
11. Shaftesbury [62]	£60	11. Bath [78]	212
12. Cirencester [66]	£58	12. Glastonbury [80]	209
13. Bruton [68]	£55	13. Torrington [93]	173
14. Bath [78]	£45	14. Ilminster [97]	165
15. Glastonbury [85]	£42		
16. Barnstaple [89]	£38		
17. Bodmin [93]	£37		

23 Wells in context in the 1524–5 Lay subsidies

Figures on the left ranking in the South West region. Figures in square brackets on right national rankings in top 100 towns after *Cambridge Urban History I* pp 761-7.

Turning to the details, the vast majority still paid on goods (*24*). Only 55 paid on wages and they represented 5 per cent of the wealth. Nobody paid on rent. At the lower end the Wells return is unusual in that nobody paid on goods worth the minimum £1. The local assessors seem to have been shielding those with few possessions. The distribution of wealth was most uneven with the top six payers controlling 40 per cent and the top third 84 per cent. In contrast most were very humble. Some 25 per cent paid on wages and 44 per cent on goods worth £2. It is interesting to relate guild membership to wealth (*24*). Only half of those worth £50 or £200 thought it worth joining. Between £4 and £45 it was usual to join and members formed a majority over all but also at every individual sum except £20 and £5 where there was an even split. Those with goods worth £3 or £2 or relying on wages must have found the costs of membership a major deterrent. Over half never joined, while many of those worth £2 who did join did so later presumably when their fortunes had improved. But it should be noted that some guild members did not pay. Three members held minor offices in the period 1523-5 but do not appear.

Assessed wealth	No. paying	No. free before 1524	No. free later	% free at any time	No. of women
ON GOODS					
£200	2	1	–	50	–
£50	4	2	–	50	–
£45	1	1	–	100	–
£40	2	2	–	100	–
£30	2	2	–	100	–
£25	1	1	–	100	–
£20	4	2	–	50	–
£16	5	4	1	100	–
£13	7	4	3	100	–
£11	1	1	–	100	–
£10	7	4	1	71	–
£8	4	1	2	75	1
£7	1	1	–	100	–
£6	5	4	–	80	–
£5	4	1	1	50	–
£4	11	6	3	82	1
£3	9	3	1	44	–
£2	98	25	11	37	4
Total all assessed					
On goods	166	66	21	45	6
ON WAGES					
£2	9	–	1	11	–
£1 13s 4d	1	–	–	0	–
£1 6s 8d	16	–	2	12	–
£1 3s 4d	1	–	–	0	–
£1	28	–	1	3	–
Total all assessed					
On wages	55	0	4	7	0
COMBINED TOTAL	221	66	25	42	6

24 Wells payers in 1524

Those worth £200 or £50 lived in High Street with one exception. He was the clothier John Mawdeley who lived in Chamberlain Street, in the house formerly occupied by John Attwater. He had been admitted as a freeman in 1492. He paid a fine as an outsider and was somewhat older than average on admission, having been born in 1458. He was the son of Sir Richard Mawdeley who, in 1494, purchased one of three manors at Nunney. John was already one of the elite in 1497. He served as master on six occasions between 1508 and 1531. His prominence may be related to a marriage to the Attwaters. But he contrasts with John Attwater in seeming to be less personally involved in the cloth trade. Attwater's will was full of legacies of appropriate commodities such as woad or equipment. For example, his great pan (probably a dyer's vat) went to Mawdeley. Mawdeley's will was to concern land and money. Mawdeley surrounded himself with kin. He had another John as his apprentice in the early years of the century who was probably his nephew and the heir to Nunney. The 1524 returns include a William Mawdeley who was worth £10 and unlike John it was he who had the live-in servants. Later John's cousin Richard seems to have had a similar role. In contrast, John's own son, a further John, trained in law and when he became a freeman in 1529 he uniquely paid a fine to be free of office within the borough.

The other payer on goods worth £200, Richard Powlet, and one of those worth £50, Richard Tyle, do not appear elsewhere in the town's records. Perhaps they did not spend much time in Wells. Certainly, they played no part in public affairs. The other three worth £50 are much better known. Henry Cornysh was a veteran of the guild, having been admitted in 1490, and paid £10 towards the 1497 fine. He was master three times. Walter Serger was a member of the guild elite and served three terms as each of master and MP. In contrast, William Vowell was a member of an established family but never became a freeman. His grandfather, the first William, was a merchant and nine times master. His son Richard (the second William's father) went to London and became a lawyer. He returned to Wells, became a burgess, and progressed to master after seven years. Like many lawyers he often described himself as 'gentleman'. The second William obviously took these claims to genteel status even more seriously. He never joined the guild and eventually moved to Long Ashton. His son, another William, moved even further from his commercial roots. He settled in Norfolk and in 1554 he granted the family's last Wells properties to Bubwith's Almshouse. They comprised a row of four cottages opposite it.

Such non-joiners left the guild elite dangerously small. Only ten of those assessed in 1524 ever became master. Most were worth £30 or more when assessed. The other three were firstly John Ustweyte, another veteran and only worth £16 by this time, but probably more affluent earlier. Next there was Robert Bekham, the new town clerk, also worth £16. He did not become master until 1544. So his fortunes could have improved or it could have been a special honour. The third was John Cutte who only paid on £13. He served his first term as master in 1525 so his wealth is unlikely to have changed. He is also unusual in living in St Cuthbert Street while other masters lived in High or Chamberlain Street. His selection demonstrates the shortage of suitable candidates. It also shows that family tradition could matter. John Cutte I was admitted in 1407 and achieved all the senior posts except master. Thus he was progressively rent collector, constable and MP. His sons John II and William were admitted and it was the latter who became master twice, beginning in 1444. William's son John III was more obscure but he in turn was father to John IV who was three times master and once MP. Such family continuity is otherwise unknown in the Middle Ages.

Wells still had foreign resident but they were a modest group. Three paid on goods worth £2 and the other on £3. Only one, a Sadler Street barber, became a burgess. Again only six women paid. One paid on goods worth £8, another on £4 and the remainder on £2. The days of affluent aliens and wealthy widows had passed. One group had increased and it was people of Welsh origins or ancestry. This was a recent phenomenon. The earliest obvious Welsh inhabitant was John Ryce (or Ap Rees) admitted in 1473 and the main build up was in the new century.

ECONOMIC DIFFICULTY AND RELIGIOUS CHANGE 1525–1552

As we have seen from the 1524 returns Wells had economic problems. It had two persons of great wealth and a mass of people relying on minimal goods or modest wages. The elite was dangerously small. The impact of the new tax must have depressed matters even more. The town was attracting few with the means to become burgesses. The 1520s saw freeman admissions at their lowest ebb and for a time those willing to pay the full fine, in other words outsiders, shrunk to less than a fifth of the intake.

There were also problems in the Liberty. The chapter was still troubled by absenteeism. Wolsey had surrendered the see but in 1525 he imposed his 16-year-old illegitimate son as dean. He held the post until his father's fall in 1529 but spent the period in continental travel with his tutor.

Wolsey's son, Thomas Wynter, was succeeded by Richard Woolman. In 1537 he left money to finance the replacement of the old High Cross. It was still under construction in 1543 when John Leland visited Wells. The result was a magnificent structure. There was a definite hierarchy in medieval crosses. Minor towns had market or high crosses that comprised a stepped base with a simple shaft rising from it. Lesser crosses in important towns such as Wells also took this form. More important places had the central shaft surrounded by an arched structure. The grandest crosses surmounted this with a spire-like superstructure. In Somerset only two other places aspired to this form (*25, 26* and *27*).

CONGRESBURY.

25 Congresbury Cross after Pooley. This is a basic street cross, a type used as a market cross in lesser towns, as a village cross or as a minor cross in larger towns. The Queen's Cross at Wells was certainly of this type as its stepped base survived to be drawn by Simes. The others were probably similar

However, there was again friction with the bishop. Bishop Clerk's time was notable mainly for the aggrandisement of his brother Thomas. He held the best of the bishop's leases (those for the mills) and also accumulated the first enduring private estate in the town. (The need to provide for bishops' families and the existence of private estates were to be major features of the town from 1560.) In 1539 the burgesses protested about the exactions of the bishop's bailiff. He was compelling all tradespeople to buy a license to do business. The citizens claimed that they were free to buy and sell in the borough without payment. They particularly mentioned the bakers, brewers, butchers, fishers, innholders and millers as being hampered in their callings. This grasping bailiff was in fact Thomas Clerk. Perhaps Clerk's successor, Bishop Knight, atoned by providing money for a new market house in the middle of Market Place. His bequest was supplemented by surplus funds from Woolman's legacy.

Meanwhile the Reformation was gathering pace. From 1529 to 1534 Henry VIII was basically trying to pressurise the Pope into accepting his divorce. Progressively papal jurisdiction, revenues and prerogative were stripped away. It was only with the Ten Articles of 1535 that doctrinal change began. The clergy had had to sign up to the Royal supremacy, the succession and the articles. At

26 Bridgwater High Cross after Pooley. This is typical of the arched structures used in towns of some pretensions

27 The High Cross at Wells after Pooley. The elaborate spire-like structure obviously makes a more striking statement than the Bridgwater cross. Only Taunton and Shepton Mallet attempted a (less elaborate) spire in Somerset. The best parallel is with the surviving Poultry Cross at Salisbury

Wells there were no martyrs like the London Carthusians, More and Fisher. Presumably, even Polydor Vergil signed. Certainly, documentation survives of his acceptance of the articles and later the communion in two kinds.

1535 also saw the *Valor Ecclesiasticus*, which set out the wealth of the church. The combined income of the bishop and chapter at Wells was £2,573 per annum, a massive sum compared with the assessed wealth of £1,502 10s possessed by the citizens a decade before. Furthermore, the majority of that assessment was on capital, not income.

In 1536 the smaller monastic houses were dissolved. In Wells this had little effect as only the small estates of Minchen Buckland and Minchen Barrow nunneries were involved. This merely meant that some 14 householders now paid rent to the crown. In 1539 the larger houses followed. These included the Hospital of St John the Baptist. This was more serious. The town lost a source of hospitality for travellers and a place of care for the old and infirm. Also the rents of the second largest estate in the borough (*28*) were now diverted to outsiders rather than spent locally. The transfer was peaceful, although the display of a quarter of the last abbot of Glastonbury reminded everybody of the price of opposition. There was a further drain on local resources in 1537-40 when Thomas Cromwell became an absentee lay dean.

Owner	Location			
	Borough	Liberty	East Wells	Total
a. estates which survived the Reformation				
Town Authority	113	–	5	118
Dean and Chapter	42	7	10	59
Vicars Choral	22	1	6	29
Bubwith's Almshouse	8	–	3	11
Precentor	10	–	–	10
Bishop	4	1	2	7
Succentor	1	–	2	3
Axbridge Corporation	1	–	–	1
St John's Hospital, Bath	–	–	1	1
Winchester College	1	–	–	1
TOTAL	202	9	29	240
b. estates of institutions No./dissolved 1536–47				
Hospital of St John, Wells	60	1	8	79★
St Etheldreda's Chapel	27	–	–	27
Minchen Barrow Priory	11	–	–	11
College of Montroy	7	–	–	7
Holy Trinity Chantry, Cheddar	5	–	–	5
Minchen Buckland Priory	3	–	–	3
Croscombe Guild	–	–	1	1
Morning Mass Tenement	1	–	–	1
TOTAL	114	1	9	134★
COMBINED TOTAL	316	10	38	374★

28 Leasehold estates in 1535

★ including 10 properties not located.

In 1540 an event of local significance occurred. John Mawdeley senior died at the age of 82. Leland referred to him as a great clothier and added that he had been succeeded by his son. However, we have already seen that the younger John was a lawyer. He had a busy career. He was retained by the cathedral from 1534 to 1569. He held various posts at the Middle Temple culminating in the Treasurership in 1551-2. He also held many appointments requiring legal expertise being at various times a county JP, escheator for Somerset and Dorset and steward of the Bristol sheriff's court. He was also MP for Wells on seven occasions. It may be that Richard Mawdeley ran the business for him, but he was dead by 1550. In fact the elder John was the last great merchant at Wells. Circumstances were turning against the men of smaller towns. Partly, it was a matter of changing business organisation. Transactions were getting larger and capital costs of major items such as ships increasing rapidly. This created difficulties with the rudimentary economic system. Partly, it was political as the Merchant Adventurers of London progressively obtained a monopoly of undyed broadcloth exports. London now dominated the economy and below it Bristol dominated this region. The larger Somerset towns all had to operate at a more modest level. At Bath three contemporaries of the elder Mawdeley, Style, Kent and Chapman were similarly the last major clothiers (Ponting 1957 35-6 & 51-2; Everitt 1967 565).

The local economy at Wells was to suffer further from the plundering of the bishop's estates. The bishop lost resources and fewer visitors were attracted to the palace. Immediately after its surrender the king had leased the hospital site and its demesne lands to John Ayleworth who was receiver-general for Somerset at the department established to deal with seized lands, the Court of Augmentations. The demesne lands comprised the block immediately to the west of the site and Beryl Farm. Then in 1543 the bishop was 'persuaded' to exchange his Hampshire manor of Dogmerfield for the hospital site and demesne. Dogmersfield was far more valuable and useful on journeys to London. The hospital only yielded a rent from Ayleworth who obtained a further 60-year lease from the bishop.

Ayleworth's accumulation of Wells interests continued. In 1545 he and Ralph Duckenfeld took leases of all the Wells properties of the hospital and of Minchen Barrow. The transaction lists 79 tenants for the former and 11 for the latter. Ayleworth was to renew the hospital lease for further 21-year-old terms in 1555 and 1571. He thus paid a fine to each of Mary and Elizabeth. No doubt this was a useful gesture.

By 1545 somebody of greater power was turning his attention to Wells. He was the future Edward VI's uncle, Edward Seymour first Earl of Hertford and then Duke of Somerset. Now the Abbey of Muchelney had possessed the prebend of Ilminster and with it the canonical house at 23 East Liberty. By 1469 the house was ruinous and the abbey in financial difficulty. They surrendered it and the cathedral treasurer, Hugh Sugar, rebuilt it at his own expense and gave it to the vicars choral. Now Hertford seized it on the basis of his possession of the 'late monasterye of Mochilney'. The next year Polydor Vergil was again in trouble and had to surrender all his possessions into the king's hands. Most were returned but his canonical house was lost. By the time he was permitted to retire to Italy, keeping his income, in 1550 it was in the Crown's hands following Seymour's attainder. Queen Mary leased it and Elizabeth sold the freehold in 1564 (WCA VI/24; *CPR 1549-50* 311; *CPR 1563-6* 103). After Edward VI's accession and his own creation as Duke of Somerset,

Seymour's ambition grew. He intended to build a power base in the county. He extorted first the site of the hospital from the bishop and then the bishop's palace, forcing him to remove to the deanery.

By that time more Church property was being confiscated. In 1547 masses for the dead, chantries and free chapels were abolished. In Wells the sites and estates of the College of Montroy and the chapel in Southover, together with a small estate owned by Cheddar Chantry and a single East Wells house owned by the Croscombe Chantry, passed to the Crown. In 1548 John Ayleworth bought the college site and estate while the East Wells house went to the Thynnes of Longleat with the other Croscombe Chantry properties. The chapel estate also remained a unit until the end of the seventeenth century. In contrast the Minchen Barrow and Cheddar properties were dispersed, adding a few freeholds to the local property market. The town may have gained as boroughs, unlike the Church, were permitted to keep the rents from obits and chantries so they could use them for other purposes. They thus retained income but were relieved of traditional burdens which had often become uneconomic.

On Somerset's fall the bishop's palace was returned but his other acquisitions reverted to the Crown estates. Furthermore, the loss of the bishop's manors continued through Mary's reign and into the early years of Elizabeth. By 1560 his 26 manors of 1535 had been reduced to eight. Phyllis Hembry charts this decline from a wealthy bishopric which she characterised as well up the second rank and often a stepping stone to higher appointments to a far more modest position. She sums up the bishops appointed to this far less promising position 1540-1640 as follows 'Wells seems to have become a dumping ground for aged deans (four of these), archdeacons and academic administrators (two of each)' (Hembry 1967 5-40 and 254-5).

The declining economy led to further difficulties in the property market. In about 1547 the dean and chapter reviewed their rents reducing them to more sensible and enduring levels. In 1550-1 the town did the same. The yield of its urban properties fell by over £10 or 15.5 per cent. Several shambles were written off. The estate now yielded £61 1s 10d which was 8s less than after the previous revaluation of 1427 but this smaller income was from a holding with 22 extra properties.

Three other points need to be noted from these years. Firstly, as the change to more doctrinaire Protestantism accelerated under Edward VI iconoclasm began. Inside St Cuthbert's the decoration of Tanner's Chantry and the Jesse Tree were hacked off. In the town the minor crosses with their religious dedications and imagery came under attack. Seven crosses on the approaches and streets of the town had vanished by the 1580s. Only the High Cross with its trading functions survived, apart from the base of the Queen's Cross which was portrayed by Simes in 1735. Townscape and ceremonial life were both impoverished by the losses. Secondly, these changes impacted on numbers of guild officers. Inevitably all the various Church-related posts except the churchwardens vanished as the associated altars were swept away. Thirdly, the Liberty also had its losses. Sir John Gates, the king's collector of lead, had the roof from Burnell's great hall in the palace and he blew up with gunpowder Stillington's Lady chapel in the Cloister to get at its lead roof.

THE MARIAN REACTION

The reversion to Catholicism under Mary produced no martyrs at Wells (although eight priests were burnt in the diocese). Bishop Barlow and Dean Turner were deprived but they went into exile. Turner was to be restored in 1560. In the meantime he spent time working on his *A New Herbal* published in three parts from 1551–68. It was to earn him the description of 'the father of English botany'.

There were protests. Thomas Lygh (or Leigh), at that time a servant to Dean Turner, came into St Cuthbert's and burst out 'What the Devil have we here? Are we going to set up idolatry again?' at the sight of a picture of Jesus between two candles on the High Altar. He was imprisoned but soon released. This escape was probably due to the legal skill of the younger John Mawdeley. Certainly, this was alleged by James Fitz James whose family seem to have been on bad terms with the Mawdeleys. Mawdeley himself was no strong Protestant. Cromwell had listed him as an MP opposed to the Act for the Restraint of Appeals (to Rome) and his public career had faltered in Edward VI's early years but flourished under Mary.

There were changes. The canonical house in Market Place became a seminar to train new priests. But the property settlement was not challenged. Too many vested interests had been created and the government needed the income from sales and leases. In fact Mary confirmed the town's possession of what had been various obit rents.

This period saw the establishment of charitable funds that indicate economic distress. In 1554 the master of choristers, Richard Bramston *alias* Smith, bequeathed £100 for a rotating fund to aid ten youngsters. Then in 1558 Walter Cretynge, Archdeacon of Bath, left £60 for a fund to aid poor burgesses. The latter is two years before a similar scheme at York which David Palliser regarded as early for its kind (Weaver 1905 154; HMC *Wells* ii 707; Palliser 1979 86).

ESTABLISHING A NEW ORDER 1559–1603

Generally, town economies began to improve in the second half of the century. Ultimately this growth was fuelled by a rising population. In fact the earliest signs appeared in Wells just as the institutional estates were reducing their rents. In 1547 no less than 14 freemen were admitted, half by fine and two described themselves as esquires. This was the beginning of an upward trend while numbers of outsiders willing to pay to become burgesses climbed back to 40 per cent. From around 1560 rents began to improve and by 1584 town rents had reached the level existing immediately prior to the 1550 reductions. However, it was a modest improvement. For reasons already discussed Wells was never again to have men of the stature of Peter le Monier, Thomas Tanner or John Mawdeley senior. The days of great Wells merchants were gone and in future it would only have traders and craftsmen.

By mid-century the nature of trading had also changed. The Tudor and Stuart period was the great age for inns. More people were travelling for trade. Alan Everitt described these inns as 'the hotel, the bank, the warehouse, the exchange, the scrivener's office and the market-place of many a private trader' (Everitt 1967 559–61). Deals that were still made in the open market were often confirmed in an inn. The boom in Wells' inns is clear. The buoyant early fifteenth century saw two more, the vicars' Christopher or New Inn at 35 High Street in 1404 and the town's Swan in 1422. There was nothing more until the last 20 years of the century. The Mermaid is first mentioned in 1487 and both the Antelope and Cornish Chough in 1490, while the Hart's Head was built in 1497. The first half of the sixteenth century saw the addition of the Star, Katherine Wheel, Crown and Bull while the Antelope, Swan and Christopher were rebuilt. The second half of the century saw the addition of the Red Lion, Ash in the Well, Black Bull, Three Horseloaves and Saracen's Head. The best sites were now clear. Most clustered around the Market Place–High Street–Sadler Street intersection so that they were close both to the market and the Liberty. Failing this, the next best site was on the edge of town where the tired and thirsty could be intercepted. The Black Bull (later the White Horse) at the western end of Southover and the Saracen's Head at the head of New Street are examples of this (*colour plates 25 to 28*).

Besides the boom in inns, the townscape changed in one dramatic way. The central tower of St Cuthbert's collapsed. Presumably it had been weakened by earlier rebuilding. In 1561-2 the town arranged a collection for the new roof. It raised £55 of which £38 came from High Street verdery.

The absence of merchants left a vacuum in the power structure of Wells (and other Somerset towns). Into it moved people describing themselves as 'gentleman' or 'esquire'. There had been a few fifteenth-century merchants who had so described themselves at the end of their career. One was John Sadler who, in one of the many pardons necessary after a change of fortunes in the Wars of the Roses, was dismissively described as 'John Sadeler of Wells gentleman *alias* merchant'. We have also noted that the lawyer Richard Vowell styled himself as a gentleman.

From 1547 the description of gentleman or esquire regularly appears in the freeman lists. They were a mixed batch. Some were from families of country gentleman who were now prospering as prices of foodstuffs, particularly grain, had improved relative to other commodities. Also it was now customary for them to be trained in law. Younger sons would then practice in it rather than be sent to a town to take up a trade (as with John Mawdeley senior) or put in the church (as with his kinsman Thomas). So the gentry moved to Wells partly for social life, partly seeking election to Parliament and also because both town and cathedral offered lucrative legal careers. Others were trying to establish themselves as gentlemen. A good example is John Ayleworth who had built up a local estate and served as MP. The bishops' kin and major officials provided further elements. Finally, it became more common for successful traders to look for genteel status in later years and to educate their sons appropriately.

The younger Mawdeley largely withdrew from public life after 1559. He kept some legal work but increasingly, adopted the style of a landowner. He abandoned his father's leases of houses and shambles in the town. His only lease was of Butt Close, which adjoined his Chamberlain Street mansion. The 1569 muster certificates show him the best equipped inhabitant. By that time he had acquired rural manors as he is described as esquire. He died in 1572 and his son, who played no part in public affairs, soon followed him ending, the Mawdeley connection. Bishop Clerk's brother Thomas and Thomas' son, William, kept up a presence in Wells although the latter built a country house on the site of Minchen Barrow nunnery. They added to the developing social life of Wells but they played no part in town affairs.

The main influence in town affairs was now the Godwyn family. They had been founded by John, the successful fifteenth-century glazier. Descent may then have been through the female line as the freeman admissions record three successive John Godwyns, *alias* Lenges. Fortunes also dipped. The John assessed in 1524 had goods worth £10 and only progressed to churchwarden. The next John was a mercer and revived family fortunes. He was master four times and MP twice. His son William turned from trade and became surveyor of the bishop's lands. Thereafter the family regularly call themselves gentlemen but unlike the Vowells they remained in Wells and played a role in town affairs. Thomas Leigh had also prospered, serving as master or mayor on five occasions. In his later years he called himself a gentleman.

There was also change in the Liberty. Dean Turner's three successors were absentees. All were laymen trained in law who took the income but rarely, if ever, visited Wells. The second, Valentine Dale, held the office while serving as ambassador to France. He sued his predecessor's executors over the state of the deanery but then allowed it to become ruinous. He then purported to sell it, assuring the chapter that this was for 'the good of the church and the better setlinge thereof of the dean and his successors'. The chapter protested to Archbishop Whitgift and Lord Burleigh whose pressure led to promises of redress. In fact Dale left things unresolved so that the first two resident deans in the new century, Haydon and Meredith, were faced with challenges and ultimately a law suit.

Wells lacked a resident dean from 1569 to 1602. The office of subdean became important and its income was boosted by combining it with that of the succentor, who had a small estate to support him. The subdean and his colleagues had to deal with a continued shortfall in income. Economies were sought. In 1560 Torgate was demolished to save on repairs. The accounts were put in better order by transferring some properties from the impoverished escheator to the better-placed communar. This probably happened around 1569 when John Danne held both posts.

Bishops now possessed less income but often had a wife and children to consider. Their support had to include provision after the bishop's death. Consequently there was an impact on both Church offices and landholding. Bishop Godwin (1584-90 and no relation to the Wells Godwyns) established an enduring pattern. He had five sons and three daughters. Two sons became canons at Wells while a third was made parson of Kingston Seymour. One canon, Francis, went on to become bishop first of Llandaff then Hereford, but Paul remained at Wells. In 1587 the bishop's eldest son, Thomas, and his son-in-law, Thomas Purefy, received the lease of the two great mills together with other property.

The town guild (which was in improving circumstances) was aware of the weakening position of the bishop. He had lost income and influence. In addition the spread of more extreme Protestant ideas meant that he was no longer sure of general respect. The town began to exert itself in the time of Godwin's predecessor, Bishop Gilbert Berkeley (1561-81). In 1566 he complained on three counts that:

1 they were keeping the Three Weeks' Court for the burgesses use in dispute between themselves;
2 they were attempting to take a bond of tailors for the reformation of apparel;
3 they were sitting around the High Cross when the bailiff read out notices and proclamations rather than standing respectfully.

The town replied that it would not give up any order which had been customary. They then proceeded to breach custom themselves. In 1571 they decided to build new meat and fish shambles in the middle of High Street. Almost simultaneously they resolved to redeem the lease on 28 High Street and to convert it to a linen market. Next year they resolved to build a new town hall over the fish shambles. In 1573 they further formalised arrangements for their own internal courts and at about the same time they closed off Horse Lane to build a small tenement next to the Christopher. The bishop's prerogatives over the land of the manor, markets and jurisdiction were all under attack.

Late in 1573 a commission was sent down to Wells to hear the competing claims. Inevitably the evidence showed the burgesses to be encroaching on the bishop's rights. The guild obviously hoped for a new charter of self-government. In 1578 they had a charter but it merely confirmed existing rights and privileges. After this, they seem to have at last faced up to the fact that they would only succeed if the bishop was suitably compensated.

We have a picture of the town at the end of Bishop Berkeley's episcopate in the tax return for 1581-2. Surprisingly, Wells ranked as top town in Somerset in all of total assessed wealth, number of payers and sum paid. This must reflect the general collapse of town economies rather than modest improvements in Wells since 1550. The tax was levied on either rents worth at least £1, or goods worth at least £3. As a result payers were fewer than in 1524 at 101. Also as a result of both genuine decline and a now universal understatement, wealth had fallen to £434. In Wells nobody admitted to goods worth more than £20 (and only three other towns in the county equalled that sum). Ten persons paid on rents compared with none in 1524. Most striking is the number described as esquire or gentleman. There were three of the former and 15 gentlemen. The esquires comprised William Bowerman, a lawyer, William Clerk and Richard Godwyn, son of William the bishop's surveyor. The gentlemen ranged from successful traders such as Edward Bevill who paid on £20 and Thomas Llewellyn to include two more Godwyns, Alexander Towse a lawyer and Richard Bourne a nephew of the former bishop. Three of five payers in the Liberty were gentlemen in contrast to the 16 servants who had paid there in 1524 and of whom only one had exceeded the minimum £1. Alienation of houses and some leasing was changing the character of that area from a clerical enclave.

The arrival of the needy Bishop Godwin gave the town an opportunity. After some three years of negotiations the bishop gave his consent. The path was smoothed by a payment of £100 and the promise of £10 for each of the three following years to the bishop's son Thomas. The way was clear for a radical new charter and it came in 1589. The guild was transformed into a proper borough corporation and Wells was stated to be a free borough or city.

The town was now to be governed by a common council of a mayor, seven other masters and 16 capital burgesses. The 24 were responsible for selecting the mayor for the coming year and for filling any vacancies in their own numbers. They also appointed the recorder and town clerk, who often served as capital burgesses, plus two sergeants at mace who were lesser men and not councillors. In addition the old posts of constable, rent collectors, churchwardens, shambles, conduit and street wardens were retained and the financial arrangement strengthened by the addition of a general receiver.

The town now had its own court presided over by the recorder with the mayor and one other (usually the previous mayor) acting as local JPs. It was to have its own gaol in distinction to those run by the bishop and the dean and chapter. The council could make enforceable by-laws. The letters patent make it clear that these included a monopoly on trade providing 'no one who is not a burgess shall follow their art, mystery, trade or occupation…before they have a licence of the master and wardens of their trade'. Previously becoming a freeman of the guild was not essential. Now burgess status was vital to anybody of ambition and the trade companies had real significance. Membership was necessary if one wished to function in Wells in any business.

There were seven of these companies which seem to have been evolving by the 1490s but which were not listed until 1555. They comprised:

1 the hammermen;
2 the cordwainers;
3 the butchers who took in others dealing with animal carcasses, that is glovers, tanners and chandlers;
4 the weavers who included dyers and (strangely) barbers;
5 the fullers who included shearmen and cappers;
6 the mercers who included most of the victuallers;
7 the tailors.

These bodies rarely became involved in economic regulation. Instead they provided social functions, breakfasts (provided by new members), feasts and drinking sessions. They also organised displays in the ceremonial year. Now they gained a role with potential political power. This was later to lead to friction.

John Aish was the first mayor and William Bowerman (the unofficial recorder of the 1570s) the first recorder. They and their successors were supported by a small elite. Members were often connected by marriage and many had links to landed families, usually those of modest means.

In this period the property market reached a new equilibrium. In the period 1563 to 1576 the government disposed of its freeholds. First to go was 23 East Liberty. Within the year the vicars had bought it back. Next was the archdeacon's house. Then in 1574 Christopher Hatton received the site of the hospital and its demesne lands. In 1576 Roger Manners, Esquire of the Body, received the remaining hospital lands. By 1600 all the hospital properties were reunited in the hands of the Dodington family of Breamore, Hampshire, although they only assumed full control as the Ayleworth leases expired. Meanwhile, in 1569, John Ayleworth had sold the site of the college which changed hands twice more by the end of the century. However, the Ayleworths retained the George and the other college possessions until the end of the seventeenth century.

There was another adjustment in property as a result of the 1589 charter. The town needed its own prison. Its first attempt came in 1591 when one of the two shops under the new town hall was taken in hand and converted. In contrast the bishop no longer needed a prison for townsfolk. It had been known as 'Le Cage' and stood on the narrow strip between Sadler Street and the precinct wall. By 1595 it was replaced by a shop rented at 6d per annum (PRO SC6/Eliz/2008).

By 1600 the problem of repair to leasehold properties was nearly solved. By that time the dean and chapter and the vicars had switched mainly to leases for three lives although the dean and chapter preferred 40-year terms for their best properties such as the New Works. These leases put the burden of repairs squarely on the tenant who also counted as owner for purposes of taxation and rates. If they sublet they would further have the problem of vacancies. The institutions were opting for low profile ownership. But there was a price. As the tenants had more burdens, rents froze. The levels of the late sixteenth century mainly persisted to the nineteenth. In theory owners could reclaim rising values from the fine, the lump sum paid when taking a lease. In fact this did not happen. Wells fines only began to increase in the eighteenth century. The corporation was slower to change. By 1600 just over a third of its leases were for three lives. Part of the problem was that leaders of the elite both before and after 1589 were prone to grant themselves long-term leases. For example, in 1558 William Godwyn took an 80-year lease on a large house in Chamberlain Street and various minor properties. Similarly in 1590 William Bowerman received a 76-year lease of 76 High Street. Therefore most change was after 1605.

There were two more reorganisations by Elizabeth I. The chapter and vicars each received a royal charter in 1592. The chapter's charter put administration of the cathedral and its lands into the hands of the dean and eight canons rather than in the wider body of diocesan canons. The number of vicars was cut to fourteen. As they could now marry, that meant that each vicar was entitled to two houses in the Close. This left a surplus which could be let.

Finally, it should be noted that the bishop's financial position improved sharply in the final years of the century. Lead production on Mendip was peaking and the bishop benefited. He also used his considerable administrative ability to maximise returns from his estates. He could resort to doubtful expedients to support his wife and son. The canonical house in Market Place was vacant in 1598/9 and Still seized the opportunity to grant a new lease for the Crown and its two neighbours which was to be assigned on his death first to his wife and then to his son John. The unfortunate tenants were caught between John Still and the new incumbent, John Young, in the period 1613–22. It is not surprising to find the Yards, the tenants at the Crown, in the emerging puritan party.

$$7$$

CONFLICT 1603-89

INTERNAL CONFLICT 1603-11

The period from the accession of James I to the flight of James II was characterised by conflicts driven by religious divisions. Wells saw an early parade of differences in a dispute about traditional ceremonies. It revealed how the corporation was splitting between puritans and others. Part of the difficulty was the small size of the elite. This was well illustrated in 1602 when Thomas Baron, a linen draper and already over 50, became a burgess and capital burgess. Three months later he became a master and mayor within a year. His brother Henry soon followed him into the ruling group. Baron was sponsored by two of the leading members of the council, the lawyer Alexander Towse and Leonard Crosse, and he had been apprenticed to William Godwyn. So he was very acceptable to this group. But they could not always be selective and had little choice but to take willing persons of means. As a result a new faction developed within the council.

The most active of the new men was John Hole, who described himself as a maker of cloth and worsted hose. He claimed to keep 500 poor people in work although given the town's population this seems exaggerated. He became a burgess in 1597 and was churchwarden in 1598. He soon showed his difficult temperament. In 1599 he quarrelled with a master, William Williams, and was discommoned when he refused to withdraw his 'opprobrious words'. He appealed to higher authority in the form of the Lord Chief Justice, Sir John Popham. Under pressure the council gave in but Hole refused to be reinstated until satisfied in other disputes.

He was to be supported by Hugh Meade, a pewterer, John Yard, a hatter who also kept the Crown, and Humphrey Palmer, a grocer. In addition the group had some backing from John Aish, the first mayor.

Tensions were already high in early 1607 when Hole launched an attack on another capital burgess, the barber surgeon Edmund White. But the triggers for what followed were decisions to hold a church ale and a full set of summer shows. All traditional ceremonies were now under attack from a combination of pressures. Puritans detected both Catholic and pagan elements in them. Also they saw them as encouraging drunken and immoral behaviour. Capitalist businessmen saw them as distracting workers for long periods and the ruling class was suspicious of anything that threatened law and order. In 1594 the Somerset JPs had used a poor harvest as an occasion to ban church ales. Therefore the mayor Alexander Towse would not agree to the churchwardens' proposal telling them that they must seek sanction from county justices. They approached Sir John Rodney of Rodney Stoke and Pilton who now owned the Mawdeley mansion in Chamberlain Street. He refused but consent was obtained from the dean, Benjamin Haydon. He was a relatively inexperienced man in his first major appointment.

It is worth running through the sequence of events as they give us an opportunity to see what the traditional cycle must have been like as it ran from May Day to Midsummer's Day. On Friday 1 May a party set out to bring in the May starting before dawn. They were accompanied by a drummer. As they made their way down the street, Hole, who was serving as constable, ordered them to go home. He was defied by one of the group, Stephen Milliard. Milliard was a tailor, kept the Ash in the Well and also served as one of the sergeants at mace. As a result the group continued and set up the maypole by the High Cross and danced around it until about 8am.

Sunday 3 May was the critical day setting the tone for what followed. Dancers were out from about 5am with their drummer. After an hour the street warden asked them to stop. When they refused Hole appeared and ordered them to disperse. He was obeyed and it was peaceful until after morning service. The main proceedings then started. It was unfortunate that Hole lived at 41 High Street facing its widest portion before it was much reduced by middle row (*29*). As a result he was likely to be exposed to the maximum disturbance. Indeed a picnic was held in this area and one of two bowers for musicians erected nearby. At about 1pm the serious dancing began. It was to be led by the Maylord, George Greenstreet, and his more mature partner, Thomasina White, the wife of

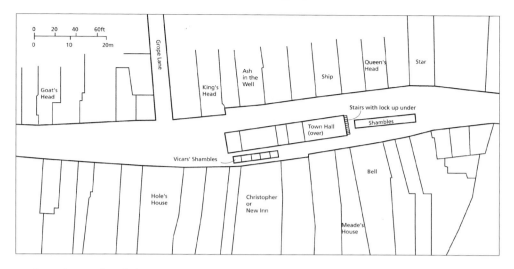

29 Central part of High Street, 1607

Edmund. Her husband and John Gilbert, a gentleman from East Wells, were chief dancers. They were accompanied by two fiddlers, a taborer and two drummers.

Hole intervened trying to arrest the fiddlers. He was confronted by another master, William Watkins. Their argument repeated national debates on the nature of Sunday. Was it a day apart for prayer and contemplation or were sports and pastimes allowed outside of the hours of divine service? The fiddlers were arrested but escaped or were released. Hole tracked them down, playing cards at Milliard's during service. They were rearrested and again freed. After the evening service the dancing recommenced. It was a processional dance and when they reached Hole's house the dancers became frenetic. Subsequently, they had to pass to the north of middle row as the way to the south was restricted to single file. Here they collided with Hole. He, of course, could have gone by the south side. The dancers then went on to Gilbert's house apart from Thomas Petters and a drummer who circled Hole, bating him.

Yard's wife, Anne, claimed that she was unable to go to church as the maypole, which she described as a painted calf, stood in her way. She was being over-nice in as much as the Crown had a rear access and she could also have crossed St Andrew's Churchyard and gone via Chamberlain Street. On Sunday 10 May she got a response. Edward Cary, who was Morris Captain and also involved in the local militia, procured a board painted with the picture of a calf. In the afternoon this was paraded down the street by men armed with muskets, pistols, swords and daggers and accompanied by drums, fifes and trumpets. They were then joined by morris dancers performing with rapiers and daggers. On several

30 The Crown Inn from a photograph taken between the World Wars. It had changed little from 1607 when it was at the centre of the events of 10 May. Note also the Red Lion, also an inn by 1607, but then with a different facade, and the Crimea cannon which stood there for over 80 years before being melted down for munitions in the Second World War

occasions they gathered outside the Crown (*30*). After a gap for evening service the activities continued until dark.

Thursday 14 May was Ascension Day and the children's pageant. Hole only managed to take exception to the fact that some mothers missed church preparing their children. The processions occupied both the afternoon and evening and were escorted by Cary and his group, now armed with halberds, bills and pikes. The following Sunday was quiet until 6pm when Cary and some 30 young men returned from a church ale at Croscombe. They danced the morris until Hole and two deputies arrived. His attempt to arrest the tabor player provoked a struggle, but evidence differed as to who struck the first blow and who pushed whom into the gutter of running water. Later Cary's group disrupted Hole's instruction of the nightwatch and left noisily when ordered to disperse.

Whitsunday, 21 May, saw more morris dancing and Trinity Sunday, 31 May, more elaborate entertainment. Hole again complained of people missing church to prepare their children. After morning services the drummer summonsed the people and various shows were performed, particularly the story of Robin Hood. Again Cary's armed troupe escorted the procession. After evening service the shows resumed.

There followed a pause until the week beginning 15 June which witnessed most of a series of shows put on by the four verderies of the city and East Wells. The shows also seem to have been associated with the different trade companies which were (or had been) located there. Monday's show came from Tucker Street and was associated with the fullers and shearmen. A parade featured giants and meat for the master's supper while the show told the story of the Pinder of Wakefield. Tuesday saw the High Street show. Dean Haydon allowed some of the cathedral choristers to sing at the head of a procession featuring supper meat, a giant and giantess, the majority of masters and many tailors and shoemakers. Wednesday belonged to Chamberlain Street which produced the most sophisticated display. The procession had at its head a show of Diana and Actaeon with choristers dressed as nymphs. This was followed by leading corporation members, Sir John Rodney and the schoolmaster William Evans all on horseback. Various shows followed interspersed with groups of morris dancers. The shows included George slaying the dragon and 'Prince Arthur and his Knight'.

Thursday was the day for the Southover show. This was designed to ridicule the puritans. Five horses were involved. On the first was Thomas Bison, a miner. He had a brush in one hand and a hat in the other with more old hats at his belt. He shouted that he had as good hats to sell as Yard. He was followed by Matthew Lancaster, a husbandman, dressed as a woman with a spinning wheel. He represented Hole's wife or employees. As he passed Hole's house he cried 'More worsted Mistris!' Next was John Smith, another husbandman, with a saucer on a plank which he beat with a hammer and other pewterware on his belt. He shouted he had pewter as good as any of Meade's. The fourth horse carried James Lideard, a butcher, impersonating Palmer and accompanied by Gamm an apprentice as Palmer's clerk. The normal company show included St Clement and a friar dispersing grain. In parody Lideard had an old bag full of trash which both flung at the crowd crying that Palmer had no such raisins in his shop. The fifth horse had a double load. William Torre represented a usurer and Robert Atwell, a chandler, his scrivener. Their cries implied that the four puritans needed money but that their credit was poor. Intermixed with all this was a more traditional impersonation of old Grandam Bunch. Meade was so furious when he saw the show that he seized Smith's hammer and tried to drag him from his horse. Hole went to the mayor but neither he nor Sir John Rodney offered real help.

A break then followed as it was fair time. The last show came on Friday 25 June and was presented by East Wells. Hole, Yard and Meade were again ridiculed. A board a yard long was painted with likenesses of Mrs Yard and on either side Hole and Meade. A second board was set at right angles. Along it balls could be trundled towards nine holes below the figures. William Gamage carried the 'Holing Game' on horseback, rolling balls with cries of 'He holes it for a Crown' to which the crowd responded 'He holes it not by a yard' or 'If you need hole go hole it in a mead'. Gamage also shouted 'Holing is against the king's proclamation', no doubt parodying Hole's references to James' proclamation on Sabbath observance. The basic reference was to allegations concerning Hole's relationship with Anne Yard, a matter later investigated by the Church courts.

Hole now went to London to complain to Bishop Still who had been away. As a result the bishop's bailiff arrested Gamage and other obvious participants such as Bison. Gamage passed the time by composing a libellous ballad attacking Hole's party. It was widely circulated. In September a second, anonymous, libel appeared.

Bishop Still died in 1608 so Hole decided to go to the Court of Star Chamber. His petition cleverly linked the incidents in Wells with rebellion in Northamptonshire and Catholicism. He had some reasons for the second. Gilbert had been listed as a recusant in 1597 while James Godwyn (head of the senior branch of the family) was discommoned for recusancy in 1602. Hearings extended over two years and Hole won. The general run of his opponents were imprisoned in the Fleet prior to being pilloried in London, then sent down to Wells to be pilloried again. They were fined and ordered to pay Hole compensation. White had to pay a double fine and Gamage was whipped.

Hole had gained the immediate victory but it cost him political power in Wells. The corporation was not overthrown and he never held office again. He began to miss meetings only returning when about to be discommoned. Finally, he stayed away long enough for them to replace him in 1613. Yard died in 1614 but Meade and Palmer went on to have long careers and serve as mayor. However, Meade remained a difficult man to work with and both were involved in financial abuses discussed below.

All this gives the impression that all the town was against the puritans (or for a frolic). However, an event in 1610 shows that the puritans could also produce rowdies. A Chamberlain Street resident, Agnes Vernon, erected a private maypole at her door. She was abused and threatened by a group in which wives played a vocal roll. It is striking that only one servant was from nearby. The others had come some way to be affronted by the maypole.

The other feature of these years was the corporation's attempts to provide buildings for its new duties. In 1603 it proposed to build a pesthouse to accommodate plague victims. The passing of the outbreak and financial difficulties left the project unrealised. The financial problem was not in rents, which were still increasing, but in fines. As a result a survey of properties was undertaken in 1605. After that there were no more long leases to members and the switch to three life terms quickened. The next project was more successful. The first attempt at a gaol had proved inadequate. In 1606 it was agreed that the tenement forming the western range of the modern City Arms should become the common prison. In 1611 it was made more secure.

RELATIVE CALM 1611–1640

After this crisis the ruling group tried to preserve a show of harmony, although it was to be marred by financial scandals. However, we can begin with some more positive events. In July 1613 Bishop Montague wrote informing the corporation of a coming visit by James I's wife, Queen Anne of Denmark. He asked two things. Firstly, that they purchase a silver bowl for her. Secondly, that the streets be made handsome and cleared of beggars and rogues. The response was enthusiastic. The streets were to be pitched (paved) with particular attention to Sadler Street as they were meeting her at Brown's Gate. Also the company shows were to be revived for her entertainment.

On this occasion the shows were carefully managed, being overseen by Recorder Southworth, James Godwyn (who had been reinstated in 1610) and Thomas Coward. The shows were as follows although it is unclear as to whether items were tableaux or small plays. First came the hammermen. They presented their streamer or banner followed by Noah building the Ark; Vulcan at his forge; Venus carried in a chariot with Cupid on her lap; a morris dance and finally a dragon. Second came the tuckers with their streamer. Third were the tanners, chandlers and butchers. Their main item was a cart of old virgins arrayed in leather, cows tails and horns. They were followed by St Clement and his friar distributing alms and Actaeon and his huntsmen. Fourth were the cordwainers. They presented the standard shoemakers show of St Crispin and St Crispinian followed by their streamer and a morris. Their expenses came to £6 1s 6d. Fifth were the tailors with their streamer and a show on the story of Salome and John the Baptist. Finally, there were the mercers who were again the most elaborate. They had their streamer followed by young children performing a morris; a giant and giantess; King Ptolomeus and his court under attack by the dragon; St George and his knights coming to the rescue; and Diana and her nymphs in a chariot with Actaeon turned to a stag.

This was the final traditional parade. It also shows the changing fortunes of companies. The weavers did not appear and were obviously in decline. The innkeepers would soon replace them as the seventh company. Again the tuckers managed only a banner and were also in difficulty. A clothiers company was established in their place but did not last.

This period saw more ambitious efforts to deal with the problems of the poor. As described there were bequests to boost employment in Mary's reign when good works were back in favour. Subsequently, the Elizabethan Poor Law meant that from 1572 a rate was collected to be distributed by the guardians of the poor at St Cuthbert's. This may have kept starvation at bay but did not provide new jobs or shelter for the infirm. From 1589 new bequests began to address these issues. In that year, Thomas Leigh left the residue of his lease of a Priest Row cottage so it could provide a home for a poor old man. This was followed by £30 left by William Bowerman to buy coal for the poor and £50 from Lady Anne Sharington for the poor of Wells. These funds, those left by Brampton and Cretynge and other money left for more general purposes were usually lent to burgesses for two year terms at 8 per cent interest and this income spent on poor relief. Bishop Still's death provided the first opportunity for a larger scheme. After some discussion with his son Nathaniel it was agreed that £500 be used to help the poor already in Bubwith's Almshouse and also to add accommodation for a further six.

In 1614 a larger bequest followed. Henry Llewellyn left £500 down plus a further £100 after his mother's death to provide a new almshouse. Unfortunately, the council did not immediately invest the money in hand to endow the new house. Instead it too was used for loans. Most went to councillors at only 6 per cent and without securities. This abuse may explain why James Godwyn decided to benefit the poor without involving the corporation. In 1618 he left a substantial house on the sites of 6–12 St Cuthbert Street and with a large rear garden on Beggar Street (to be bought for the churchyard extension in 1801). It was to pay £10 per annum to the poor. A third was to go to Bubwith's Almshouse, with a third to the churchwardens and the remainder to be distributed by the proprietors of the house.

In 1621 the corporation exchanged properties with Stephen Milliard to gain possession of the yard and stable adjoining the prison so that a workhouse for the poor could be established. Nothing happened despite a further resolution in 1623. Part of the problem was Hugh Meade's refusal to play his allotted part in supervising the scheme.

There was a further scandal in 1626. The corporation was required to maintain supplies of gunpowder and match. In this year Humphrey Palmer and Henry Foster sold powder to the hundred's militia. They failed to account for the money immediately and the dispute dragged on for years.

Eventually, in 1629 the council decided to buy land at Wedmore to support the new almshouse. This decision was triggered by the death of Mrs Llewellyn which released the last £100. They agreed to pay £700 but prolonged their loans by paying in three instalments. They nearly defaulted on the payments as they were so bad at either paying interest or returning the capital. The worst offenders included the mayor Thomas Baron, the new recorder John Baber and Hugh Meade.

The final payment for the land was made in 1632. By that time they were under double pressure. Baber was instigating proceedings about 'misemployment of money given to pious uses' while Llewellyn's heirs were suing them for £108 12s missing as a result of the low interest charge and an alleged £70 overpayment for the Wedmore land. No doubt these cases also explain the decision to provide a burling house over the prison where boys could be employed removing knots (or burls) from cloth. In 1636 Llewellyn's Almshouse was finally established on a corporation owned site in Priest Row.

After this experience the final scheme was dealt with quickly. Walter Brick proposed an almshouse for four in 1636. Within a year a site in the garden of Bubwith's almshouse was agreed with the dean and chapter. The combined Bubwith's, Still's and Brick's complex was often know as the Old Almshouse from that time. It was to remain in that form until 1777 when a final four places were added by Edward Willes on behalf of his late father Bishop Willes.

In contrast to their doubtful record elsewhere the corporation acted admirably as regards its estate. There were no more long leases after 1605 and in 1614 they resolved that a member wanting a lease had to 'absent himself from the company' while it was discussed.

As regards the property market as a whole, rents were now stable with one exception. The boom in inns meant that their rents were increased. The Swan was let for £1 16s 8d in 1550. By 1605 this had risen to £4 and in 1642 it was £10. This trend continued until the Restoration, when the vicars' Christopher reached £11 7s and the Ash in the Well (created from the town's linen market in 1599) rose to £6 2s 6d. Ownership also settled down. In 1611 James Godwyn bought the estate of the hospital thus returning a substantial income to the town. His heirs held it until after the Restoration although a portion was sold to William Prowse who also established a presence in Wells. In contrast the actual hospital site was retained by Sir William Dodington and was to pass by marriage to the Lords Brooke, later Earls of Warwick. The college site changed hands frequently until 1611 when it was bought by the schoolmaster William Evans whose family held it until 1752.

The 1629–35 volume of convocation book ends with the note 'my lord chief justice would have but one alehouse in the town'. Economics dictated something different. Inns continued to increase with the Bull's Head licensed in 1600, the Flower de Lis and Queen's Arms both described as newly built inns in 1606, the

King's Head called a new inn and the Bell first mentioned in that year, the Ship in being by 1610, the Three Cups licensed in 1620, the Hare and Hounds leased as an inn in 1635, the White Lion and the Goat's Head in being by the 1640s. This abundance of good inns helps explain why the quarter sessions at Wells were attended by more magistrates and went on a day longer than other sessions. As the corporation now had oversight of lesser drinking places, we know something of these. In 1635 six tipplers (beer sellers) were listed in Tucker Street verdery, five in Chamberlain Street, seven in Southover but none in High Street. In 1636 Richard Heale provided sureties that he would observe 'the articles of alehouses'. Five of the tipplers were widows while the others were mainly operated to provide supplementary income. John Edicot who ran a house in Southover was a shoemaker and also served as sergeant at mace for six years. His business was larger than most as he was also reported as a tobacco seller together with innkeepers, vintners and apothecaries.

After five brief episcopates Bishop William Piers arrived in 1632. Like Still he was a good administrator and arrived accompanied by his family and senior staff. His auditor Arthur Mattock founded a gentry family that lived in Wells for a century. Piers' affluence can be judged by the Ship Money return for 1637. He paid £2 out of a total of £12 levied in the Liberty. The dean contributed £1 6s 8d and the canons sums between 10s and 15s except the precentor who paid only 2s 6d. The clergy together paid over 60 per cent of the levy and no layman paid over 6s 8d.

Piers had one other characteristic which was to make him enemies in both the laity and some clergy in Somerset. He was a keen follower of Archbishop Laud and vigorously promoted his reforms.

Apart from the religious reforms and Ship Money, Wells was little changed by Charles I's direct rule. Ship Money was levied on nine named Somerset towns. Taunton was assessed at £100, Bath and Bridgwater £70, Wells and Minehead £60, Ilchester, Axbridge and Yeovil £30 and Langport £20. Other places contributed to the county levy of £7,520. Comparisons with 1581-2 and 1641 suggest that Wells did rather well and this was helped as the Liberty contributed £12 (despite objections from the hundred). Nevertheless, it, like other places, experienced increasing difficulty in collecting successive levies.

There were two opposing social trends in this period. The poor had to cope with the final collapse of broadcloth production. The elite prospered and were ever more 'gentrified'. This is illustrated by the Subsidy payment of 1641 and the Protestation return of 1642 which are further described below. In 1641 two of the payers are described as esquire, 29 as gentlemen and two others as 'Mr'. In 1642 the classification is rather different. The term gentleman is only used in the Liberty where the canons and vicars are called 'Mr'. Here there were fourteen gentlemen compared with six in 1641. In the rest of the city there were no gentlemen but there was one esquire and 52 individuals called 'Mr' including all those classed as gentlemen the previous year and still present.

They were a mixed lot. The Godwyns were of course a local family who had prospered. They were now represented by the younger James Godwyn who was a recusant and therefore excluded from public affairs. Their major role there had passed to the Cowards. John Coward, a yeoman from West Pennard, had married Thomas Leigh's daughter and heiress. Their son Thomas Coward married the daughter of William Watkins who was mayor three times. Thomas was prominent in town affairs from 1610 and lived in the mansion on the south side of Chamberlain Street. His children form different marriage alliances. The elder, Thomas, married the daughter of the bishop's chancellor while William married into the country gentry.

Several were lawyers. John Baber, Alexander Jett and Tristram Towse were the principal law officers of respectively the town, the bishop and the chapter. Some were descendants of cathedral dignitaries, such as Samuel Powell son of Dr William Powell. Others were bishops' kin or officers. For example, Ezekiel Barkham had arrived as Bishop Lake's receiver and stayed to serve four successors. Country gentlemen were also moving in. We have seen that the Rodneys had a base in Wells. In addition, William Prowse, a member of the Compton Bishop family, took the Protestation as a resident in the Liberty. If gentry did not move in themselves, the town was obviously seen as a suitable place for their widows. From 1609-17 Margaret, the widow of Sir Henry Berkerley of Bruton, lived at 17 East Liberty. In 1641 Jane, the widow of Bishop Bourne's nephew Roger lived at 18.

Finally, there were senior traders such as the elderly Baron brothers who styled themselves as gentleman on the strength of their service as mayor and local JP. However, the Barons never made a permanent transition, which is in contrast to the Cowards. Traders might also feel the traditional pull of a country estate. The wealthy woollen draper William Bull purchased the rectorial manor of Shapwick, the tithes of Ashcott and the manor of Sydenham for his son. Nevertheless, the family retained Wells properties and links. His grandson Henry served as city MP and JP after 1660.

The other striking fact apparent in 1641-2 is that Wells was a centre of Catholicism. Only 12 Catholics were listed in 1597 and most were women. This had now climbed to 38 evenly divided between the sexes. It was the biggest concentration in Somerset. Some were local families, the Beomonts and Godwyns which had both split into Protestant and Catholic lines. Others had arrived as office holders but their widows or descendants were recusants. William Evans, the schoolmaster, had left a Catholic widow and son. So had John Lunde who arrived as keeper of the palace under Bishop Berkerley and held the post until 1635. It was unfortunate that Anne Lunde continued to occupy accommodation in the palace as this must have inflamed puritan suspicions of Piers. In fact the majority of recusants lived in the Liberty. They included two new families of gentry status, the Canningtons and Cottingtons.

WAR AND COMMONWEALTH 1640-60

The disintegration of Charles I's regime began with the wars with the Scottish Covenanters. This necessitated the calling of the English Parliament. Wells sent Sir Edward Rodney and John Baber to the Short Parliament. For the Long Parliament they replaced Baber with Sir Ralph Hopton. This replacement marks the final stage of the souring relations between Baber and the council. He resigned as a capital burgess soon after and did not attend convocation for over three years. The Wells MPs were initially in accord with the other Somerset members. All felt the need to limit royal power and were opposed to Bishop Piers. It was only later when the more extreme Parliamentarians threatened all royal power and the established Church that they split.

Citizens would have seen an immediate difference with the resumption of Parliamentary taxation. In early 1641 a new Lay Subsidy was taken. It was followed by a graduated Poll Tax. Then came news of the Catholic rising in Ireland. Parliament took an oath to support the Protestant religion, the king and Parliament. It was ordered that all men should take this Protestation or have their refusal noted, and that was done in spring 1642. Parliament had by then turned back to fund raising. As the previous levies had disappointed they followed the precedent of Ship Money. A fixed sum was allocated to each county to be divided by commissioners. It was then up to places to raise it, subject only to set lower limits.

The survival of these four documents is patchy for Somerset. For Wells only a damaged 1641 Subsidy roll and the Protestation return survive. But by combining what survives it seems that Wells was the most populous town in the county but exceeded in wealth by Bath and Bridgwater.

The 1641 return is a sharp contrast with 1581-2. On this occasion 58 persons paid on land compared with 26 on goods. Of the former 37 paid on the minimum value of land, £1. This was a tax avoidance tactic as they only paid 8s compared with a minimum of 12s on goods. Wealth was grossly understated. Nobody paid on more than £5 worth of goods or £6 worth of land. Families such as the Barons or Cowards who had obviously prospered by combinations of advantageous marriages, property acquisitions and low interest loans admitted to less wealth than the previous generation. James Godwyn junior paid on land worth £4 while the hospital estate was actually worth over £60.

The Protestation return lists 869 adult males. In the Liberty there were 13 vicars, 43 other signers and 4 non-signers. In the rest of the city (for Tor Street is certainly included) there were 801 signers, 18 non-signers and 10 officials. All these should be about a third of the population, suggesting a total of 2,647 people. The most striking point, if the two lists are compared, is that the population is already becoming highly mobile. Many who paid in 1641 were not in town in 1642. Absentees include Baber, Tristram Towse and the grazier Ralph Sinox (or Cinox). The first two reappeared but Sinox vanished. In 1649 he could not be traced. The cathedral dignitaries were also largely missing. Bishop Piers was in the Tower and only his son William, the treasurer Dr Creyghton and the schoolmaster signed.

By August war was imminent. Sir Ralph Hopton, the Lords Hertford and Paulet were in Wells with the royal commission to raise forces for the king. The pro-Parliament mayor, Robert Morgan, thought it expedient to present Hertford with an ox. On the hills above town a rival body under Sir Francis Popham, John Horner, Richard Cole and William Stroud were raising a force for Parliament. They had more popular support and the tactical advantage. The Royalists withdrew. The corporation now presented the Parliamentary general Lord Bedford with a hogshead of claret. The Parliamentarians did not occupy the town which was left open to raids by Parliamentary troops drawn by the cathedral and palace. In October rumour of an attack resulted in a deputation of four councillors being sent to Glastonbury to confer with the Parliamentary officers. There was no raid but in April and May 1643 Parliamentary troops did indeed loot and damage the palace and cathedral. But fortunes were changing. The Royalists united their forces and drove the Parliamentarians back across Mendip. The advancing troops looted Wells and the town found that it had a demanding master. In August the corporation had to bow to Hertford's demands and expel Stephen Haskett and Robert Morgan. This breach of unity troubled members. The mayor Robert Rowley went to visit his imprisoned predecessor, Morgan, who accepted the situation without taking offence at his colleagues. The resolution removed him 'until it be further considered', thus hinting at later reinstatement. In that month William Saunders, David Barrett and Anthony Taunton were disenfranchised as burgesses for being in arms for Parliament. The only corporation members known to have fought were William West (Morgan's replacement as master) and John Niblett who were both royalists. Far more citizens were involved. West wrote of his regiment being full of Wells men. The able-bodied were liable to be swept up by either army.

Worse was to follow. The corporation wrote to Hopton requesting the removal of his violent and demanding postmaster, Joseph Nurton. Hopton's response was to billet Prince Maurice's regiment on them. Financial exactions increased, £100 to Maurice in April 1644 and £500 to the king in July. There were also demands in kind for shoes, stockings and horseshoes. West's replacement as mayor, Robert

Casebeard, was a shoemaker and took advantage of the opportunity offering to provide 200 pairs of shoes if the corporation paid.

Within two months of Nurton stabbing a street warden, the churchwarden Thomas Brinte, had murdered Thomas Foster, one of the masters. Unfortunately, we lack the evidence to know if this related to wider struggles or to some private dispute. Certainly, society was increasingly violent.

In August the Parliamentary General John Middleton moved into south Somerset. Wells received his demands for horses and bridles plus £300. There was a veiled threat. If the town complied it would be protected from plunder. The corporation played for time by querying the division of the sum with the hundred and Middleton moved away. At that stage our records break. The chapter obviously ceased to function but convocation books break off from September 1644 until October 1662. One suspects that a volume was 'lost' soon after the Restoration to save members embarrassment.

From other records it is clear that Wells like all Somerset was becoming increasingly restive at Royalist demands and lawlessness. When the king's officers arrived from Bristol to levy excise, Mayor Casebeard refused to publish the proclamation. One of the masters told the officers that he would pay no excise and another that they came to rob and devour the people.

Then in July 1645 Fairfax led the New Model Army into Somerset and smashed the Royalists at Langport. From 28 July to 2 August the New Model was at Wells demonstrating its superior discipline. Somerset had changed hands for a last time. At Wells Royalists such as West were removed. Morgan and Haskett were reinstated while the Republicans Thomas Meade and David Barrett joined the corporation. The last on his tax returns and property holdings would not have risen so far normally. But a broad continuity of membership was maintained. The recorder, Christopher Dodington, survived until 1655 although he was the brother of the violent Royalist officer Sir Francis Dodington and was himself investigated in 1645.

Somerset was now governed by a county committee and this in turn was controlled by John Pyne of Curry Mallet. He packed the committee and other bodies with his supporters. Morgan became a committeeman and Barrett one of its associated officials. He was the marshal and in charge of prisoners. Later Morgan became a county justice and Meade was placed on the county grand jury and assessment committee. This new group soon alienated the county. Tax demands multiplied. There was a weekly assessment to pay and excise. Power was abused. Barrett provided the most sensational example. He had Dean Raleigh in his charge. In 1646 the dean refused to show him a letter he was writing to his wife. Barrett then stabbed him with a sword or dagger giving him a fatal wound. Barrett was never called to account for this murder. Nevertheless, Pyne held on to power until Cromwell seized control in 1654.

In 1649 we have a picture of Wells from the Parliamentary surveys of confiscated church lands. It reinforces the picture of population displacement. Some 45 per cent of those holding such properties had not been in the town in 1642. Some had left and now returned. Notable amongst them was Daniel Tuthill, who had given evidence for Hole in 1607 and in 1614 had leased a Chamberlain Street property for three lives. He was away in 1642 but the 1649 survey found him in possession. He claimed to hold the property as the last life of the 1614 lease but could not produce documentary proof. So he had lost his papers at some stage. Some had vanished, for example Ralph Sinox. A few were abroad. Robert Creyghton had followed the future Charles II into exile. John Davy of East Wells, an ostler's son, was also 'beyond seas' perhaps as somebody's servant. The other cathedral dignitaries were scattered. Bishop Piers was in retirement at Sunbury-on-Thames while his son William worked in the cheese markets at Taunton and Ilminster. Most of the canonical houses were in new hands but Mrs Creyghton was still in possession claiming tenancy in her husband's right but without proof. Her father, the royalist William Walrond of Isle Brewers, leased a house nearby. One wonders how they got on with their new neighbours.

The surveys included estimates of improved rents. These show the rents of the precentor's, vicars' and dean and chapter's properties were on average 428 per cent behind market value. As we have seen fines failed to compensate for this shortfall. As a result those with the capital to pay the fine could make a good profit by subletting at a rack rent. A class of *rentiers* was appearing. Nine men now held three or more leases. The largest block was controlled by the former bishop's registrar Alexander Jett. The number of women holding property also temporarily increased. Only 12 held on their own lease while 20 held on deceased husband's or father's leases. One other change in land use was recorded. For the first time an inn was established in the Liberty. It was the Decoy Pool (later the Fountain) sited on the East Liberty-St Andrew Street corner. The sign was only relocated to its modern site, c. 1810.

At this time Cornelius Burges arrived in Wells. He was an eminent Presbyterian divine who had loaned large sums to Parliament. Now he was compensated by the post of preacher at the 'Upper Church in Wells' (the cathedral) and possession of the palace and other Church property. He actually lived in the deanery. He demolished parts of the palace, selling some of the materials and using others in the deanery. He divided Gunthorpe's hall to two storeys of low-roofed rooms. He tried to exploit his new estates to recoup his money. As a result he was soon in dispute with the corporation. To make matters worse he assumed ownership of the bishop's canonical houses, leasing or selling them although they were not included in the sale.

The corporation united against such an outsider. They had bought the bishop's rights in the fairs and other of his interests in 1648. They bought the houses in 1655. This venture involved the unlikely pair of Barrett and Recorder Dodington working together. The corporation purchase of bishop's rights resulted in a decade of litigation with Burges. Both parties tried to stretch what they had bought. One case will suffice for the unlucky purchasers of the houses. Burges 'sold' Tower House to Cornet Samuel Bridger of the New Model Army for £150 and he altered it to establish a malt house. In 1655 he had to pay the corporation a further £150. He sued Burges at the Chard assizes and was awarded £700 for interruption to the malting business and because Burges refused to refund the purchase money. For one of the houses the corporation had other plans. This was the canonical house in Market Place. Burges had 'sold' this to Colonel John Dove. The corporation converted it, under Barrett's supervision, to 'a public room and a house for the reception of the country at the time of the assize and sessions'.

Barrett had a second reason to pursue Burges. As a Baptist he opposed his Presbyterianism. He led a group to London which persuaded the Council of State to order Burges to surrender the Chapter House to them for a meeting house. Wells now housed even more extreme religious groups including Quakers and Ranters. So when Burges complained to the quarter sessions about people walking and making a noise in the cloisters while he was preaching, one is left wondering who was involved. Was it Ranters, Baptists (then notorious for interrupting sermons), supporters of the old order, or were all making common cause? Probably Royalists were the least likely. What little support Burges ever got locally often included William Walrond.

Barrett and Morgan had lost their wider powers in Somerset with Pyne's fall in 1654 but they remained important in Wells. Under Cromwell the county landowners returned to power in the county and the quarter sessions resumed their primary role. In Wells broad continuity was maintained but local families had less resilience. Thomas Coward the younger had had to compound for serving as a lieutenant colonel of militia and being with the king at Exeter. He had to pay £160 and never took up his family's usual role in local public life. At the opposite pole for both town and county Henry Barlow paid just 6s 8d.

One encouraging development occurred in these years. In 1654 Margaret Barkham, the widow of Ezekiel, provided money for a new sort of charity. It was a school to educate poor boys. Initially, it was located in Bubwith's Almshouse and took 14 pupils. It was the beginning of what became Wells Blue School.

RESTORATION

The return of the monarchy brought with it a restored church. Its confiscated lands were returned involving heavy losses to the corporation and other purchasers. Cornelius Burges left Wells to pass his last five years in poverty.

Bishop Piers returned at the age of 84 while Dr Creyghton was rewarded for his loyalty with the post of dean. The two did well out of fines due for new leases and appointments. It is to their credit that much was spent on the cathedral and its surrounds. Piers spent £400 on ornaments and utensils for the cathedral and £5,000 on repairing the palace, while the dean contributed towards repairing and restocking the library. At about this time the bishop purchased the former archdeacon's house from Humphrey Walrond for £1,000. It was to be a home for his son William and his heirs, but initially William was to accommodate the bishop's second wife in part after the bishop's death.

Many of the canons had to repair their houses. Indeed two of the bishop's canonical houses lying to the east of the Rib were never put into order, although collations to them continued under the names of the west and east ruins.

Corporation records begin after commissioners appointed under the Corporation Act 1661 had purged it. Barrett had already left. He needed a new start where his record was unknown. Only a further six members were expelled, notably Thomas Meade and Haskett (again) plus the town clerk, Thomas Standish. Initially, the new mayor and recorder, George Walrond and John, Lord Poulett, were outsiders, former royalist officers and men of standing in the county. They were linked to Wells by property interests. The new masters were William Coward and the bishop's son John. So the majority of sitting members were acceptable moderates and once again broad continuity was maintained. Walrond was soon replaced by local men, first the younger Tristram Towse and then William Coward, while a local deputy recorder carried out Poulett's duties.

The market house needed rebuilding. Presumably it had been neglected in the disputes of 1649–60. The new bailiff must have come to an agreement with the corporation. They provided most of the money and were rewarded with a new town hall in the upper floor. In addition the lower floor was to be used for the assizes which were permanently transferred from Chard in 1667. This lower area was adapted by placing screens between the columns to cut it off from the weather and the market. The corporation raised the money through the trade companies, presumably because their purchases and battles with Burges had involved loans and raids on the charity funds. The first meeting after records resumed shows concern about funds. Three years later in October 1665 they were still pressing the companies for money so the hall could be finished for the coming assize. The arrival of the assizes certainly helped the town's traders. At the end of the century Celia Fiennes arrived while they were sitting. She found the town full and the streets lined with stalls.

However, the difficulties with the hall and the disaster with the purchase of Church lands frightened the corporation. They did not attempt another major development until 1754. Instead, they quietly managed their estates, letting them by three life leases.

Corporation politics were also quiet. The frenzy of the Popish Plot produced a Whig faction in Wells but no major disturbance. The main influence in the town was that of the Cowards. The second Thomas had died in 1660 and his three sons had followed by 1665. The family influence therefore passed to the descendants of his brother William. William's son, another William, was educated in law, often being referred to as Sergeant Coward from his legal rank. He served as deputy recorder for John Poulett and was subsequently recorder for 40 years in his own right. He also served as MP on seven occasions. His mother had been one of the Somerset Dodingtons and he also married into the landed classes first to Bridgett, daughter of Sir Thomas Hall, and then to the dowager Lady Mohun. He boosted the family's landed credentials by purchasing the manor of Glaston and land at Butleigh.

We can see more of the opposite end of society from this time as more taxation records survive. Unfortunately, we have only exemption certificates for the Hearth Tax but the poor rates survive from 1674-5 and those who were exempt from the former were equally exempt from this rate. Also, and helpfully, East Wells is rated with the town rather than the rural areas. As a result we learn of 547 households which included about a quarter occupying rooms in a larger property. Nearly half were too poor to pay either of the taxes and only High Street verdery had a majority of payers. In addition far more women are visible. They head 20 per cent of households although they feature as only 10 per cent of lessees so most were subtenants or holding on a deceased husband's lease. In fact 82 per cent of the women are described as widow. Most were in poverty particularly the widows (31). Only High Street verdery housed an appreciable number of comfortably placed women.

Exemptions from taxation			
Verdery/tithing	No. of households	Households exempt Poor Rate & Hearth Tax	% exempt
Southover	92	55	60
Chamberlain St	97	56	58
High St	166	14	8
East Wells	110	83	73
Tucker St	82	61	74
TOTAL	547	269	48

Women and poverty 1674-5								
Verdery/tithing	Households headed by women		Women described as widows		Women exempt		Widows exempt	
	no.	%	no.	%	no.	%	no.	%
Southover	17	18	16	94	13	76	12	75
Chamberlain St	24	25	18	75	22	92	16	88
High St	22	13	20	91	5	23	4	20
East Wells	28	25	22	79	25	89	19	86
Tucker St	16	20	12	75	15	93	11	92
TOTAL	107	20	88	82	80	75	62	70

31 Taxation and poverty 1674-5

The aged bishop retired to Walthamstow and died there in 1670. His two successors were both being rewarded for services from 1642-60. First Robert Creyghton's years of exile with Charles II were recognised. He held the see for only two years but in the period since his return he had managed to entrench his family in the Liberty. In 1674 his son, Robert II, became precentor, a post he held for 60 years. Bishop Creyghton was followed by Peter Mews whose services had been military and wore an eyepatch over a Civil War injury. He was to take up arms again after his move to Winchester, fighting Monmouth's rebels and using his coach horses to pull the royal artillery. His successor in 1681 was of a younger generation. The next three bishops, when young, had adhered to the Anglican faith while it was persecuted under the Commonwealth. As a result the piety and intellectual life of the Liberty was to improve sharply.

It was in Bishop Mews' time that Wells gained its first nonconformist chapel. In 1674 Peter Cooke, Thomas Collins and members of the Sevior family took advantage of a relaxation of the law against Protestant dissenters. Cooke acquired two tenements in Southover belonging to the manor of St Etheldred's chapel. Two years later the new building on the site was registered as a Presbyterian church.

The first of the younger men after Mew was Thomas Ken. He had gained Charles II's respected by a public and principled stand against the royal mistresses. However, his friend Samuel Pepys thought his sermons 'weak' or 'forced meat'. He was the bishop who attended Charles in his final illness. He attracted comment in Wells by his custom of dining with 12 poor people in the palace.

In his later years Charles II had overcome the Whigs and worked to secure his family's grip on power. One method was to grant the corporation's new charters which actually increased royal oversight. Wells was not exempt. The council was in future to comprise the mayor, seven aldermen and 16 councillors. The king had the power, when acting in privy council, to remove the mayor. The first mayor was to be Richard Hole, with David Trym as town clerk and Thomas Wyndham as recorder.

REBELLION AND REVOLUTION 1685–8

The quiet tenor of life in Wells was shattered by the accession of James II. But again our knowledge is limited and the relevant volume of convocation book is missing. Presumably, it too could have embarrassed the elite later.

The town was on the fringe of Monmouth's advance as his main force went through Glastonbury and Shepton Mallet. However, they fell back by way of Wells, reaching it on 30 June. The houses of some wealthy citizens were looted and Mrs Creyghton paid the rebel Commissary General £20 to save the canonical houses from sack (the chapter later repaid her). There were stories of damage to the cathedral but it is difficult to discover what was involved. The sacrist seems to have hidden the ornaments and plate except for a silver verge.

After the battle at Sedgmoor the town soon saw evidence of the retribution to come. The Wiltshire militia passed through the town on their way home and paused to hang some prisoners. Subsequently, prisoners were accommodated in the cathedral, St Cuthbert's and the Bishop's Barn resulting in substantial cleaning bills and a claim for over £63 for their feed. Bishop Ken chose to accompany Monmouth on the scaffold. The town witnessed even more butchery when the assize arrived. At least eight men were hanged, drawn and quartered in Wells. David Trym, now county clerk, was rewarded for 'weedling' confessions out of prisoners. Ken returned to spend much time with the prisoners.

Bishop Ken was at the centre of events in 1688. He was one of the seven bishops who refused to read James II's Declaration of Indulgence in church. They were imprisoned but the celebrations on their acquittal showed how the popular mood had swung against James.

William III's invasion and the fall of James did not directly affect the town but in 1689 it had its hated new charter quashed. It was to be governed under the terms of its 1589 charter until 1835. However, it lost its bishop. Ken came into conflict with a third monarch when he refused to take the oath of allegiance to William and Mary as he felt bound by his previous oath to James. He was deprived and eventually had to be ejected in 1691. He did not forget Wells. In 1712 he left half his books to the cathedral library.

8

TOWARDS A GENTEEL WELLS
1689-1750

The previous chapter was full of characters who could be summed up as difficult. They were self-assertive, intolerant, conscious of their own rights, often self-righteous and quick to anger. John Hole, Hugh Meade and John Baber are obvious examples. Now attitudes begin to change with what Peter Borsay described as the Urban Renaissance. People began to take more interest in the arts and society placed more value on courtesy. Politics lost much of its violence although it preserved a tradition of strong invective.

Inevitably, the change took time. There were to be two riots before political life finally settled in Wells. Similarly, the Wells physician Claver Morris (*32*), whose journal informs us of so much in the period 1689 to 1726, is a transitional figure. On the one hand he loved music – devoting much time to the local music society, was interested in architecture and subscribed to a life style of travel, dining with friends and reading. But on the other hand he had a hot temper and was particularly liable to get into disputes on property and politics.

Unfortunately, space constraints mean that we cannot tell his full story here. For example, his daughter made a clandestine marriage and was disowned. She was only forgiven when she, her stepmother, Morris' lady lodger and all the maidservants burst in on the Doctor early one morning when he was still dressing to beg for forgiveness. If you want more than this outline and much other information you must read the journal (Hobhouse 1934).

32 Claver Morris. The fiery little doctor as portrayed in his memorial effigy. Now in the east cloister, it and many more were moved out of the cathedral in the nineteenth century

FROM REVOLUTION TO GREAT STORM 1689–1703

Two minutes of 1689 need reporting. First the corporation resolved to let 'the city gaol commonly called the Rainbow' to John Alexander at £4 10s per annum. (*CB IX* 20). This was the first sign that the gaol complex now included an alehouse (but not the intended workhouse). If one had to feed the prisoners it made sense to offer food and drink to others. The rent is also remarkable, the third highest charge by the corporation. Furthermore, this site alone was let short term for one-to three-year periods. Of course, what was being let was the right to exploit the prisoners. By 1701 the taker was paying £6 and from 1706 this had increased to £7. By 1701 the old Ash in the Well had become the Three Kings and its earlier name was transferred here. It was variously called the Ash in the Well, the Town Arms or the City Arms, all of which could describe the same pictorial sign (*colour plate 31*). This farming of the prison continued until 1760.

The second reported a resolution of the chapter. It began by noting the two ruins east of the cathedral and continued 'whereby there are or may be want of houses in the Liberty for canons resident...that the mansion house formerly a canonical house now set out for a terme of years...shall be made a canonical house againe'. This is strange as it uses a loss of houses in the bishop's gift to justify increasing the dean and chapter's supply. In fact, it was the beginning of a scheme by the precentor, Dr Robert Creyghton II, to get his son, Robert III, made a canon residentiary. He was able to move as he had two son-in-laws on the chapter besides himself while a third member was in debt to him. This Creyghton faction was to trouble Bishops Kidder and Hooper and to lead to a breach of the conventions of Wells leasing, with Sergeant Coward as the victim. The precentor's immediate intention was to obtain a canonical house for his son who already had a prebend and was the schoolmaster. Coward had taken over the lease of 17 East Liberty and expended a considerable sum in improving it. When he asked for a new lease an impossibly high fine was demanded. But the plot then began to go wrong. Coward stripped out the new panelling and transferred it to his Chamberlain Street mansion. The chapter had to pay to put the house in order, supplemented by £80 from the precentor, before it was fit for his son to lease. Furthermore, the scheme stirred up so much resentment that it defeated the wider purpose.

The year 1691 saw the appointment of the new bishop. He was Richard Kidder who had gained a reputation as a preacher in London. He was doubtful about accepting and it took a second, royal, request to persuade him. He was a conscientious and hard working bishop but his time in Wells was not happy. The diocese had been attached to the saintly Ken so any replacement was likely to experience resentment. Also he was too confrontational in his attempt to deal with the power of the Creyghtons. On top of this he quarrelled with Claver Morris over the Doctor's surreptitious wooing of his daughter. Finally, his health was poor.

In 1694 and 1695 there were unusual disorders. The earlier was occasioned by the bakers and other shopkeepers refusing to accept tin farthings as payment. This left the poor unable to buy. The corporation reprimanded the bakers and ordered them to accept the coins. The 1695 incident was triggered by the visit of the Quaker, William Penn. He preached to a crowd, said to exceed 2,000, from an upper window of the Crown or its neighbour. Mayor Matthew Baron had him arrested only to discover that the bishop was more liberal and had licensed Penn.

In 1699 we can see how the Wells property market normally worked. Claver Morris had obtained an assigned lease of the dean and chapter's house at 19 East Liberty. He now began to build himself a new house in front of the old. It took two years to build and cost him £807 14s 6d. He obtained his own 40-year lease in 1702. He renewed this in 1720. At that time it was realised that the boundaries had been wrongly described. As a result Morris had built a wall on his neighbour's land. He accepted the principle but took offence as he was not compensated for his loss. It provoked a typically outburst. He sent a message to the dean and Dr Archer that he 'wish'd they would have acted Honestly this once: but, I must look on them as two egregiously unjust and knavish Rascals to keep my Wall which cost me more than 40s'. Nevertheless, his descendants by his daughter, the Burlands, continued to lease the house until the death of J.B.Burland in 1803. The house was remarkable for its use of the new sash windows on its front although, as *colour plate 22* shows, the sides had traditional mullioned casements. At about the same time the south front of the deanery was re-fenestrated, creating a pattern of apparently eighteenth-century windows in a medieval wall, which reminded Nicholas Pevsner of early Georgian experiments in Gothic. Dean Bathurst was a friend of Christopher Wren who may have been involved in the scheme.

In 1703 the Great Storm brought down the chimneys on part of the palace. They crashed through the roof and killed the bishop and his wife in their bed. Kidder was succeeded by George Hooper who again only accepted on the second request. He agreed because his friend Ken urged him to and formally resigned the bishopric in his favour. Hooper was a considerable scholar. The antique Korans in the cathedral library came with the rest of his books. He was a conscientious bishop but more diplomatic. He was able to block the ambitions of the Creyghtons so that Robert III never became a residentiary.

SOCIAL AND ECONOMIC LIFE

This is a convenient place to consider the nature of life in this period. Wells was providing ever more facilities for the gentry or those who aspired to that status. The Liberty provided a pool of educated men of good taste. Appropriate activities were expanding. The music club provided opportunities for amateur musicians and periodic concerts with imported professional musicians. Claver Morris also belonged to a group that dined monthly. They included local gentry such as the Honourable George Hamilton but also others from out of town notably Colonel Horner of Mells. Wells had buildings that were beginning to demonstrate new styles. There were also periodic race meetings.

Persons of genteel status continued to move to Wells or establish a presence in it. The two grandsons of Christopher Dodington became well known locally. They were Peter Davis, who served as recorder for many years, and Dodington Sherston. In addition William Prowse had been succeeded by his nephew John who was also heir to the family estates at Compton Bishop and, through his mother, to the Newborough's manor at Berkley (near Frome). He married Bishop Hooper's only surviving child Abigail. They were provided by a house at the head of Silver Street and just across the moat from the palace. This was a convenient halfway point between the other holdings so they were often seen in Wells. Similarly Archdeacon William Piers' descendants maintained their house in the Liberty until mid-century.

What did this presence mean for the tradesmen? If Claver Morris is typical it may have been disappointing. He made most of his larger purchases while travelling for either professional reasons or pleasure. Clothes or the materials to make them came from London, books and the ornamental urns for his house from Bath and glass and metal goods from Bristol. His large orders of wine and spirits were smuggled. They made their way up from the Dorset coast and were usually delivered at night.

However, the inns were flourishing and peaked in the first years of the eighteenth century. Morris' journal records him drinking, dining, holding meetings of his music society, reading the news, exerting election pressure, dealing in land and seeing plays in the many inns. He regularly sat on two commissions, for respectively the Land Tax and the Sewers (meaning drainage ditches). He was also involved in a short-lived enclosure commission. The Commission for Sewers sat in the Assize Hall but the others met in inns and even the Sewer Commissioners concluded business by dining at an inn.

By this time alehouses are better recorded. One common location was close to a major inn. In High Street the Hole in the Wall was next to the Star and the White Hart was between the Red Lion and the George until 1712, when its sign was transferred to what was until then the Hart's Head in Sadler Street. Presumably, these small places accommodated footmen, grooms or coachmen while their masters stayed or dinned at the major inn. In this period there was also the Cock, Blue Bell and City Arms further west on High Street.

The other tradesman to flourish in this period was the joiner Thomas Parfitt who expanded to operate as a builder. By the later 1720s he was calling himself gentleman. His son continued the business but a century later William Parfitt was chapter clerk.

For the working class, domestic service was one major choice but manufacturing had settled down and Wells now specialised in hosiery. Daniel Defoe commented on this in the 1720s while Wells was used in the trade as a name for a type of stocking just as Tauntons and Dunsters had been used for types of cloth in earlier periods.

For the poorest there was a further spurt of charitable activity. In 1675 Adrian Hickes of London had left £200 to be invested for the poor of Wells. His only specific instruction was that there should be £1 paid to the vicar for an annual sermon in St Cuthbert's. In 1701 the trustees began to invest what was now £225 in property. Their major purchases were the Angel in Chamberlain Street and 15 High Street. Where they leased for lives they charged more realistic rents than the traditional estates. For example, they rented 15 High Street at £4 per annum compared with £2 13s 4d charged by the dean and chapter for larger 13 adjoining. On occasion they also let property at a rack rent. Next in 1704 Brittaine's Charity was established and endowed with properties in East Wells. In 1713 Bishop Hooper, the dean and chapter and other members of the cathedral founded a second charity school. Phillip Hodges built it a home on land offered by the dean and chapter. It is modern St Andrew's Lodge. The Barkham's foundation soon moved in as well, while in 1715 Hickes Trustees voted to merge with Barkham's charity. By 1730 transactions were carried out in the name of Barkham's, Hickes' and Hodges' Charity and later as the Wells Charity School.

Finally, in 1726 Archibald Harper left his house at 28 Chamberlain Street, half his garden and £500 to establish an almshouse for five poor woolcombers. With this bequest early modern charity had nearly reached its final form. There were only two more additions before the coming of the Workhouse. In 1774 accommodation for another four was added to the Bubwith's Almshouse group and in 1824 Charles' Almshouse was established for two poor women.

THE EARLY EIGHTEENTH CENTURY

Sergeant William Coward died in 1705. He was succeeded by his son, another William, but usually distinguished from his father by his militia rank as Colonel Coward. He was involved in a law suit with his brother-in-law, Arthur Mattock junior, over the share of the estate due to Arthur's wife Katherine. Colonel William followed the family tradition and served as MP in 1708-10 and 1714 but he died in that year. His heiress was his daughter Bridget. In accordance with family aspirations she had been married to the youngest son of the Earl of Abercorn, George Hamilton. His was a family with an extravagant streak. George's brother Charles created the amazing gardens at Painshill and ruined himself while George and Bridget were grandparents to the notorious William Beckford, of Fonthill Abbey fame.

George shared the family passion for building. The mansion site was enlarged by incorporating three vicars' properties (including the site of Moniers Lane) into the curtilage. The whole was surrounded on three sides by a high crenellated wall. The house was rebuilt and the gardens transformed while two Union Street cottages were replaced by stables. George also wanted a rural view. Across Chamberlain Street he obtained possession of three houses and the separate

33 George Hamilton's mansion in Chamberlain Street and his then newly opened vista to the Mendips, as shown in the Buck brothers panorama of Wells made in 1736

garden plots behind them. The site was cleared and laid out to provide a vista to the Mendips (*33*). The dean and chapter were obviously uneasy about the removal of their house. In 1720 Hamilton had to covenant that 'such alterations shall be without prejudice to the dean and chapter' and that he would renew the lease after only 14 years of the 40-year term.

34 Stoberry House. Peter Davis' mansion photographed shortly before its demolition

Hamilton was not the only one interested in a grand house and grounds. From about 1718 Peter Davis began to acquire by a series of purchases and exchanges the small parcels that made up East Field. On this he built himself a new mansion, Stoberry, set in landscaped grounds *(34)*. The name was antiquarian in inspiration deriving from an earlier name of the open field which was Stabergh. A similar impulse seems to have lain behind his purchase of the Hospital estate in 1732.

Meanwhile, Claver Morris had embarked on his last great dispute in 1725. He leased two of the surplus houses in Vicars' Close. On the strength of this he claimed a right of way through the Close from his house. The vicars rejected his arguments and litigation followed. The bishop supported the vicars and was drawn into the quarrel. It was at this time that the music society had to switch location. Formerly they had used the vicars' hall, now they met in an inn.

Another change in ownership came in 1727. The old Clerk estate passed to the female line in 1621 in the form of Hammond Claxton the son of William Clerk's elder daughter. They sold it to the Gutch family who had to mortgage it. The mortgage and then the freehold came to Bishop Hooper. From him it passed to his daughter Abigail Prowse. By that time Abigail was used to estate management. Her husband had been elected as one of the county MPs, only to die of smallpox in London. She was left with an infant son and her notes in her husband's estate book show her efforts to master bundles of leases (SRO DD/CB 36). The former Clerk estate was now added and Abigail became the most significant woman property owner since Isobel Tanner.

George Hamilton found it more difficult to obtain election when he sought to follow the Coward tradition. He eventually succeeded in 1747-54 but that was after several attempts, and once having been unseated for election malpractices (a common occurrence then particularly for those likely to oppose the government). Claver Morris supported Hamilton and his journal reflects election practices. Pressure could be applied by offers of leases or threats about debts. Drink was used as a persuader. However, it might ultimately depend on the returning officer, the mayor, who could decide who was eligible to vote. Morris' journal reports his anger when many of his side's votes were ignored by Mayor Joseph Luffe in 1722.

This increasingly bitter factionalism had led to a clash between the corporation and the trade companies in the previous year. The complaint was that the companies were not producing their books for approval and were making freemen. Thus they were admitting strangers to the borough franchise. Mayor Luffe threatened to prosecute their leaders. The rival faction took to the streets. Crowds ran along the streets for several nights, armed with clubs and shouting 'Down with the bylaws!' The street wardens and constables were afraid to face them. They particularly gathered at the mayor's door. There they 'huzzaed', threatened to beat his house down and broke his windows. He claimed that he could not go out at night without a guard. This dispute flared up again in the third quarter of the century.

The Coward fortune may have been overstretched by land acquisitions and the law suit. Certainly, Hamilton's building projects plus his election expenses were too much. From 1730 there were a succession of mortgages. The first involved his brother Charles as a lender but later loans were from widowed ladies or clergymen. From mid-century the mansion had to be leased although it was not finally sold until about 1770. Family links were not quite severed. Hamilton's son-in-law, Alderman William Beckford of London, sat for Wells with Clement Tudway from 1784-90.

9

THE TUDWAY HEGEMONY
1750–1830

THE TUDWAY FAMILY BACKGROUND

Music brought the Tudways to Wells. Thomas Tudway (d.1688) had been a gentleman clerk at St George's Chapel, Windsor. His second son, another Thomas, rose to be Professor of Music at Cambridge while the fourth, Charles, came to Wells first as a chorister and then a vicar choral. The two other sons were involved in the West Indies trade. The eldest son, Clement, became a London merchant and owner of a sugar plantation at Parham, Antigua. Richard became a master mariner in the Antigua trade.

Charles married the daughter of a Wells farmer, John Robinson. He seems to have been a man with a considerable temper as he left the vicars in a passion. The Chapter Acts Book reports that in 1684 when leave of absence was denied him 'Charles Tudway, late Vicar-Choral of this church….in a discontented manner, did throw off his surplus in the body of the Cathedral Church, in the presence of Dr Creyghton…and Mr Dutton, and did also bid the receiver of Close-Hall to strike his name out of the book' (WCA Act Book 1673–1704 f.28; Tudway Quilter 1985 58-9).

This first Charles' only son was another Charles who married Mary Cook of Hay at St Cuthbert's. He was described then as a yeoman. He was a resident of East Wells for all his children baptisms except for the last in 1721, when he was described as of New Street. His earlier home was on the farm inherited from John Robinson as pew rents show (pers. comm. Anne Duncan). The family also had a property in Southover. This second Charles seems to have taken an interest in politics, as Claver Morris noted him seeking a vote for the opposite faction in 1719. His son, a third Charles, had his fortunes transformed in 1748 when he inherited his cousin's plantation (*colour plate 20*).

CHARLES TUDWAY: NEW POLITICS AND NEW ARCHITECTURE

Charles' transformed circumstances quickly became reflected in a public career. He was churchwarden in 1751, city magistrate the next year and mayor for the first time in 1755 with further terms in 1761 and 1767. He became one of the city's MPs in 1754 and sat until 1760, when his eldest surviving son Clement replaced him. This new grip on political power seems to have been associated with a series of changes, some to control more tightly the right to vote and others to improve the town.

To begin with the trading companies were disciplined, as noted members became the freemen and voters. In March 1753 the companies were summons by the corporation to produce their rules and orders. John Ball and Philip Strode appeared for the stocking makers and stated that they had none. The recorder was instructed to provide them with a new set. In contrast the hammermen needed the threat of a fine to make them comply. The outcome was an order that in future masters and wardens were to make no admissions until they had obtained the permission of the mayor and burgesses in convocation assembled. The penalty for any breach was a £20 fine.

Town improvements were certainly needed. The town was slipping as a trading centre and its textile industries were in what proved to be terminal decline. In the mid-seventeenth century it was still the largest town in Somerset. By 1750 Frome and Bath were much larger and it is likely that Taunton and Bridgwater had also outstripped it, while a number of other places (Shepton Mallet, Wellington, Yeovil, Crewkerne and Chard) were at about parity.

Marketing needed improvement. Furthermore, we are now into the stage coach era and there was a need to improve both routes to Wells and through the town's streets. In places these were now obviously inadequate for the increasing amounts and size of wheeled traffic. As a further thread, taste was changing. public slaughter of cattle was no longer regarded as an acceptable spectacle.

In 1753 a turnpike trust was established to improve the road system around Wells. It received further Parliamentary authorisations in 1769, 1769 and 1821. Besides improving road surfaces it undertook a number of route improvements, mainly to avoid steep hills. To the north the old road to Bristol had gone through Upper Milton. It was diverted to what had been the Bath road. Also this had climbed straight up Prior's and Pen Hills (as surviving tracks show). Now a new route followed the contour round the side of the hill on the line of the modern A39. To the south a similar climb over the flank of Glastonbury Tor was avoided, thus bypassing Boveton in Glastonbury. Later a new link was provided in the Northover area of Glastonbury. This shows the fate of lesser towns without their own trust. Inns and other businesses in parts of Glastonbury suffered to ease the flow of traffic towards Wells. Later, from 1830, the trust moved on to improvements within Wells as we shall see in the next chapter.

Then in 1754 the corporation began improvements within Wells with a process that was to clear, over a period of ten years, all the stalls and the middle row from High Street. The first stage was the purchase of the Queen's Arms and its neighbour on the north side of the street (modern 18 and 20). These were rebuilt with a yard behind into which the stalls could be relocated (35). The removal of the buildings of middle row took longer but as the corporation owned most it was relatively straightforward. In 1756 they made an agreement with the vicars concerning the removal of their house. They were to be compensated by an equivalent rent of 13s 4d from a corporation property. At this stage we get the only specific justification for the works which were stated to be 'for the convenience of the town and particularly the inhabitants of High Street'. As regards finance, Charles Tudway provided bridging loans. This was a traditional way in which oligarchs had had to earn their status from the Middle Ages (Britnell 1986 228-9). In addition, he agreed to purchase the rebuilt frontage properties. The corporation were further recompensed for costs and future loss of rents and fines by a public subscription. This seems to reflect some popular mood in favour of these improvements.

Charles' purchase of the Queen's Arms in 1768 was part of a wider pattern. Inns were a vital part of the mechanisms of political influence. In 1753 he had obtained an assigned lease of the Swan and in 1757 that of the Christopher. In 1768 he was granted a new lease of the Swan with no fine as he had just spent over £600 in rebuilding and repainting it. The family was to keep the lease of the Christopher until 1834. Charles' son Clement bought the freehold of the Swan in 1800 and the family did not sell it until 1885.

Charles also took action to house himself in appropriate style. The last of the Evans family to occupy the former College of Montroy, Mary, died deeply in debt. In 1752 Peter Davis and Elizabeth Shackshaft took action in the Court of Chancery. The result was an order that her heirs should sell the estate to pay creditors as much as possible. This led to an auction at the George in April 1754. Charles made the winning bid of £3,314. Then in 1758 he made a contract with

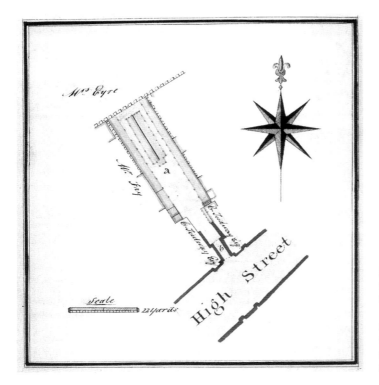

35 The Queen's Arms and the yard behind from the corporation's 1821 survey. This shows the provision made for the stalls and activities displaced from High Street

Thomas Paty of Bristol to clear the site and erect a new house (*colour plate 21*). This was to cost over £4,700. While this was going on he had obtained a small vicars' property on the east side of College Street in exchange for land at Easton. On this land the local builder Thomas Parfitt constructed Charles' stables and coach house at the cost of just over £877.

Charles took further action to improve both the interior and setting of his new home. While the house was still under construction he commissioned Gainsborough to paint portraits of his wife and himself to adorn the interior. Then, in 1761, he reached an agreement with the Archdeacon of Wells, Francis Potter, who held Tower House as his canonical house. Charles was to receive two pieces of land to the rear of Tower House in exchange for land at Dulcott. As it was unclear if the land of a canonical house could be alienated the transaction was authorised by a private Act of Parliament. This secured the view from the front windows of the new house and gave him the land with the specimen cedar trees, which were to give the house its name.

Charles also bought other land and houses in and around Wells. Some of the houses were for junior members of the family, a trend which peaked under Clement Tudway. By that time Tudways occupied four more substantial houses in Wells and the Holloways (descended from his aunt Elizabeth) and his nephew Francis Drake also had a base in Wells.

All this building activity by Charles and the corporation seems to have had a wider impact. There had been earlier examples of the newer styles in architecture beginning with Claver Morris' house and then with the grander example of Peter Davis' Stoberry House with its park. Now the pace quickened. In the period 1750 to 1820 much was rebuilt in the Georgian manner and even more given a new facade in the fashionable style. There was a contrast between the Liberty and elsewhere. The ample plots in the former meant that it was possible to follow Morris' example and go for total replacement while living in the old house. Thus in 1762 Dr Ray built behind the dilapidated canonical house at modern 9 and 11 North Liberty. Similarly around 1820 William Parfitt built his new house behind that Hugh Sugar had given the vicars. In the more cramped conditions elsewhere adaptation was more common.

A further factor in this physical renewal probably stemmed from the Act to Redeem the Land Tax. This measure included provisions for holders of long leases, such as the prevailing leases for three lives, to apply to two commissioners to set a price at which they could purchase the freehold. The government saw this as a means to improve the yield of the tax but in Wells it provided a mechanism to break the 300-year hold of the institutional estates on the property market. For example, the Corporation lost 24 properties by this procedure in the period to 1820. The takers were mainly resident gentry such as the Honourable George Hamilton and the Tudways. Most of the property sold was in fashionable New and Chamberlain Streets (a total of 15). It also included the corporation two major inns (and best rents) the Swan and the Three Kings. Acquisition was often followed by rebuilding.

It might be wondered how this activity was compatible with what has been said of economic decline. In part it was separate. The canons of Wells and the gentry who settled there drew their money from elsewhere. But even the townsfolk invested and this can be a symptom of economic trouble as capital was diverted to building projects rather than being used for business investment.

CLEMENT TUDWAY AND THE PEAK OF CONTROL

Clement Tudway sat as a Wells MP from 1760 to his death in 1815. This long service made him Father of the House. But he took little active part in its business and rarely spoke. He seems to have been more interested in the accumulation of influence than in its use.

As he progressively took over from his father he faced one major challenge to the family's power. Tension was already mounting prior to the general election of 1765. Six prominent citizens claimed the right to vote as masters of their trade companies. The corporation rejected them. Then in December an election was due to replace Lord Digby. The expected candidates were Robert Child who had Tudway support and Peter Taylor, son of Paris Taylor of Burcot then Sheriff of Somerset. The Sheriff arrived with the writ on Thursday 19 December and sent a message to the mayor, Clement's younger brother Robert, who was at his father's house in the Liberty. The initial message was that the writ had arrived and that the bishop had requested that the poll be delayed until after Christmas Day. This postponement was agreed. Next day a further note was sent informing the mayor that the precept was prepared and asking him to come into the borough to collect it. Robert replied that he was engaged with company and could not come, suggesting the sheriff called on him instead.

The result was deadlock. We cannot know whether Robert could not leave his company or was more deliberately snubbing a gathering of opponents. The result was that the writ was delivered instead to the senior master, William Keats. Subsequently, he, with the recorder's support, refused to hand it over to Robert. The result was two separate polls. That conducted by Keats and John Burland, the recorder, elected Taylor. The other conducted by Robert elected Child.

The Tudway influence was mobilised to counter this challenge and to minimise the possibility of it occurring again. Parliamentary scrutiny led to the declaration that Child was elected. At the local level Burland was dismissed and the future electorate more closely controlled, totally excluding the trade companies. A secondary result was the final decline of the companies. By 1831 the last had been wound up. Apart from their role in creating electors they had long functioned mainly as social clubs, although as late as 1761 they had retained a ceremonial role in the celebration of the coronation. The corporation voted the Woolcombers (a recent evolution) four guineas for their splendid display. Victory was incomplete in one respect. John Burland was too good and well connected a lawyer to be summarily dismissed. In February 1767 he obtained a writ ordering his reinstatement. His presence had to be tolerated for a further period.

Nevertheless, the Tudway grip on the town was now complete. It is well summed up by the *Universal British Directory* of 1783-9: 'The influence prevailing in this city is that of Clement Tudway, Esq., one of its present representatives. This gentleman has a sufficient interest always to procure a return for himself without expense and the Corporation, etc., compliment some friend or neighbour with the other seat.' Wells had become a classical pocket borough.

The main internal concern of the town was still with its relative decline. Now it faced a further threat. The courts were not housed comfortably in the market hall. Judges and magistrates were growing increasingly critical of this situation. Already in 1752 and 1756 the corporation had discussed making the courts 'warmer and more comfortable'. The loss of the assizes would have been a serious blow to both trade and prestige. By 1776 the threat was so real that the corporation nerved themselves to act. They resolved to rebuild the hall at a cost of £2,000. They offered to contribute 1,000 guineas (£1,050) if the county subscribed the rest. But they were drawn into a wider scheme while waiting for a response. In 1778 the bishop and archdeacon of Wells offered the canonical house on the south side of the market place (36). This had been isolated from the bulk of the Liberty by the building of the New Works, the Crown Inn development and Bishop Knight's provision of the market hall. Soon after the Restoration Dr Piers had used the proximity of the market as an excuse for living elsewhere. It was decided to demolish the old hall, build a replacement on the site of the canonical house and throw its front garden into an extended market place. Once again a private Act of Parliament was thought necessary to break the tenure. The new town hall was initially built on arches so the cheese market could be accommodated below.

By a further agreement the Wells Town Hall Act of 1779 also transferred the powers of the bishop's bailiff over the markets to the corporation. This had been an issue for friction ever since 1589. The corporation had last sought legal advice on the matter in 1753.

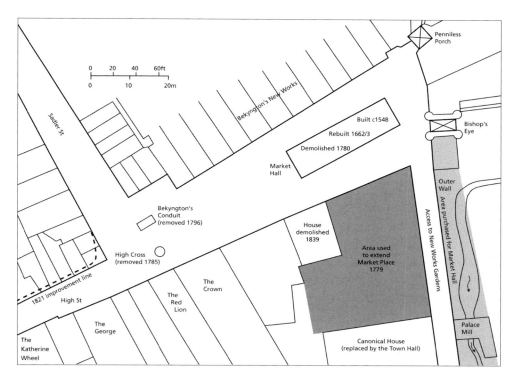

36 Market Place, Wells 1684–1839

37 Market Place, *c.*1795. This is the last view of Bekynton's Conduit which shows it settling to the north. However, it should be noted that other sketches or descriptions suggest a polygonal structure although it appears rectangular here. It is also the only picture of the front of the easternmost house on the south side which was demolished in 1839. Also note the state of the Bishop's Eye gate and the appearance of the two houses adjoining it. They should be contrasted with *48* and *Colour Plate 18.* Finally note the property on the left. This was described as newly built, *c.*1720. It was obviously constructed in a rather old-fashioned manner. Again contrast with *48*

The two medieval structures in Market Place vanished in the following two decades. In 1785 part of the High Cross collapsed. It had probably been weakened by the bailiff's efforts in 1762 to enclose part as a butchers stall and by more recent works to pave the extended market. It was removed as 'ruinous and dangerous'. In 1796 Bekynton's conduit followed. No reason was given but a picture of *c.*1795 showed it to have been settling to the north (*37*). On this occasion the bishop was consulted on the demolition and the design of the replacement erected in 1799 and still visible today.

During these years the town was also provided with new facilities. The earliest came out of Clement's 1762 marriage to Elizabeth, daughter of the Shropshire baronet Sir Rowland Hill. The family subscribed to an extreme Calvinist doctrine. As a result Elizabeth tried to establish an Independent chapel. First she attempted to revive the use of the Presbyterian chapel in Southover. Subsequently she built and endowed an Independent chapel in Grope Lane. It is the building which, in recent years, has been the chapel Bakery and then a series of eating places. By 1816 the Southover site was being used by the Methodists. It is doubtful that Elizabeth would have approved of the other two new uses. A theatre was provided on the west side of Priest Row and Polydor Vergil's confiscated house opposite the cathedral had become the Wells Assembly Rooms. It was operated by John Hayman who leased the site from the Sherston family. By 1800 he also had the 'Old City Brewery' on the site which made the group even less appropriate as neighbours for the cathedral, Vicars' Close and canonical house.

While the affluent were well cared for, the working class were suffering. The old textile industry of Somerset was collapsing in the face of the new industries of Yorkshire and Lancashire. Revd. John Collinson, writing in the last decade of the eighteenth-century, reports dislocation across the county (Collinson 1797 ii 400 & 429 and iii 13). Wells like other places experimented with silk instead. But it was not as early as Taunton which began the switch in the 1770s (Bush 1975 58) or as wholehearted as Bruton. An advertisement survives of an auction of 1828 to be held in the White Hart of:

Lot 1 Silk factory called the Palace Mill...in the occupation of Mr Johnson, Silk Throwster, held by a lease under the Bishop for three healthy lives
Lot 2 Another silk factory and water wheel engines and machinery in St Johns Street...in occupation of Jos Johnson or his tenant.

As the next chapter will show, the first of these was in poor structural condition and nothing more is known of the second. There was one other new enterprise, the brush factory founded in 1820. It was to provide much needed employment for over a century.

Another use in decline was that of the major inns. Patterns of trade were changing and fewer transactions took place in them. They were also challenged by more specialist uses. Wells had a tobacconist and coffee house by the 1730s. Now the theatre and assembly rooms removed other functions. In the second half of the century three of the major inns (the Antelope, the Three Kings and the Rose and Crown) which clustered close to the western boundary of the Liberty all vanished. Others, notably the George, were far less popular with the affluent. Lesser houses also shut, for example the King's Arms (earlier the Cock Alehouse) at 53 High Street. A minority still flourished, particularly those associated with coach or carriers routes. By the last years of the eighteenth century the Swan was the main hub, with coaches to Bath and Exeter leaving every weekday and to Taunton on three days per week. The Christopher had a further three departures to Bath. In addition the mail coaches stopped daily on route to Exeter and London. In contrast the Star was the main hub for carriers' wagons with two more services from the White Hart and one from the Mitre. Together these amounted to six departures to Bristol all returning next day, two to London leaving on Saturday and getting back the following Friday, and one to Bath. The road improvements may have helped. Certainly Wells had a better network than any where in Somerset except Bath and Taunton.

Two other points need to be made about these years. The first is that the town began to spread outwards for the first time since 1348. In 1785-6 cottages were build on what had been the wide verge on the south side of Portway. They paid small rents to the bishop as lord of the manor (SRO DD/CC 13202 nos. 255-6).

The second is to carry forward the story of the other gentry families with a presence in Wells. The extravagance of George Hamilton proved too much and he was forced to sell his mansion to Zachary Bayly of Bath. He, in turn, was ruined by speculation in development at Bath and the house then became the home of Robert Tudway. Peter Davis junior spent his later life in his father's creation Stoberry. He followed the latter's purchase of the former hospital manor by acquiring the actual hospital site and its demesne lands from the Earl of Warwick for £2,332. He also recovered from Mary Prowse various hospital properties that the Godwyns had sold to William Prowse nearly 150 years before. This antiquarian zeal enabled him to refer to his manor of St John the Baptist, Wells. He died without offspring in 1770 and his house and manor passed to his Sherston cousins. The Prowses also maintained their estates and a home in Wells. The two estates were not united until Abigail's death in 1763. Her son Thomas was noted as an amateur architect and landscape gardener. He followed his father in serving as a county MP. He outlived his mother by only four years and the estates passed briefly to his son George, and within a few months to his daughter Mary. She gave up the lease of the house called Islington in 1770 and therefore spent less time at Wells. But she kept most of the freehold estate. She married late (in 1783) and died in 1799. Her husband, the Revd. John Methuen Rogers of Berkley subsequently disposed of the properties.

JOHN PAINE TUDWAY AND THE END OF AN ERA

Clement and Elizabeth Tudway had no children, so Clement's heir was John Paine Tudway, the son of his brother Robert (the mayor of 1765). John succeeded his uncle as MP in 1815 and sat for 15 years. However, he seems to have been less interested in politics and influence than his predecessors. Also the means were failing. West Indian sugar no longer returned great profits. Its whole basis was threatened. The slave trade had been abolished in the British Empire and the campaign now aimed at the abolition of slavery itself.

John was in fact living beyond his means but the expenditure was on his house and gardens, not on political influence. He bought the triangle of land to the north of his house and bounded by New Street on the West and College Street on the east. Most of it was attached to the large house called Montroy at the head of New Street. The remaining paddock, Brandiron Close, was subsequently bought from the widow and daughters of Admiral Holloway in 1826. They had departed for Brighton soon after the Admiral's death. These purchases may help explain why he needed to borrow £10,000, later increased to £17,000, from Joseph Lovell Lovell. The security was slaves, which might seem a doubtful security by that year.

As mentioned, brush making arrived in the 1820s. Hilliers were the pioneers in 1820 and were soon followed by Parsons. Unfortunately, this was still basically a craft-made product which had to be sold at a low price. It thus offered the town neither new techniques nor high wages. The brush companies came to establish themselves in what was to remain the main industrial concentration until after 1945. It was behind the town hall where Hillier took over the eastern part of the New Works Gardens and the adjoining part of the Coneygree. Parsons was across the road in what had been an enclosure of the bishop with the discouraging name of Slovens Acre.

At first the corporation continued with its policy of town in improvements. In 1820/1 they resolved to ease the High Street–Queen Street corner by rebuilding (and rounding) the corner of the gaol (38). They also discussed the feasibility of recovering the livestock fairs moved to Priddy and Binegar at times of plague in respectively the fourteenth and sixteenth centuries. In 1821 they commissioned a set of accurate plans of their traditional estate. In that year they also commenced an even more ambitious corner improvement. This involved setting back nine properties to ease the Sadler Street–High Street corner (36). This was achieved without compulsion as all but two of the group belonged to the traditional estate. Another was purchased in 1819. The last was a small medieval property on the corner. By this time it was always held with the two adjoining corporation properties. The owner participated for £50 and new leases of these properties. Other tenants received rent rebates or new lives on their leases. However, it is worth noting that the new purchase was not let on a traditional long lease at a low rent but at a very commercial £21 per annum. A loan to finance these works came from the trustees of Llewellyn's Almshouse and not from the Tudways. Much of the cost was promptly reclaimed as the strip gained for the road was sold to the turnpike trust for £520 (SRO D/T/WEL 67). This could be seen as a recognition of a new division of responsibilities but there is a more cynical explanation. It could have been, given the overlapping membership of the two bodies, a deliberate shifting of the burden from the local community to a wider body of road users.

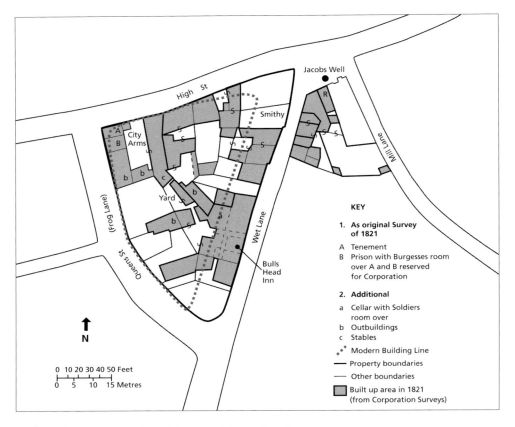

38 Road Improvements – Broad Street and Queen Street

Subsequently the corporation became bogged down in bitter faction fights as J.P. Tudway lost both the will and means to control matters. Things degenerated to a near farcical situation as meetings were fixed at dates unsuitable for the rival group, factions stayed away to prevent a quorum being reached or arrived suddenly to try to gain a majority. This culminated in a series of legal actions in 1828. As a result five members were removed and new elections ordered (WTH 72).

In 1830, as the dissolution of Parliament approached, John issued a public letter explaining that he would not stand again. He expressed the hope that this would restore harmony after the city had 'become inflamed by party zeal and imbittered [sic] by political animosities' (Tudway Quilter 1985 77). Eighty years of Tudway domination were over.

10

MISSING THE INDUSTRIAL REVOLUTION 1830-1918

ADMINISTRATIVE AND PHYSICAL CHANGE: THE 1830s

This decade saw remarkable changes and the prospect of more to follow. The old order was ending. The Ecclesiastical Commissioners (now the Church Commissioners) were established to take over the various Church estates at the next vacancy. The Reform Act of 1832 changed the franchise, while the Municipal Corporations Act of 1835 changed the nature of the corporation and extended the area of the borough to include East Wells. The town was now to be governed by a mayor, four aldermen and twelve councillors, the last elected by all male ratepayers. Internally the town authorities were still concerned with its declining status and the resultant need to provide better access and market facilities.

The commissioners who reported on constituencies before the Reform Act provide a useful picture of the town. For comparison it should be noted that the first census in 1801 had recorded a population of 2,229 in the In Parish (or borough) and 268 in the Liberty. The resultant total of 2,497 shows no increase from 1642. In 1831 there were 3,430 people in the In Parish and 381 in the Liberty. Furthermore, there were another 264 in the part of East Wells and 'fore lane' (Tor Street) in the city or Parliamentary borough. There were a further 528 in the upper parts of East Wells. So at last we have a population for the whole town of 4,613.

Population was growing rapidly. In the borough and Liberty it had grown by 52 per cent in the first three decades of the century. Housing was not expanding proportionately. The Parliamentary report also gives numbers of houses for 1821 and 1831. In the borough and Liberty population, increased by 489 or nearly 15 per cent in that decade while the number of houses increased by just 25. By 1831 the occupancy rate averaged 5.5 persons per house. For East Wells we only have figures for 1831, and there occupancy was higher at 6.6. But matters of housing and health did not as yet hold the attention of either central or local government.

There was instead a major concern with highway improvements. The turnpike trust now turned its attention to the main entries to the town. First in 1831 the northern approach was dealt with. New Street had previously forked, with the western arm lining up directly with Old Bristol Road and the eastern arm leading to what had traditionally been the road to Bath, but what was now also the Bristol turnpike. A new route was cut through Three Corner Close leading to the new Bristol road, while Ash Lane was extended to link it and Old Bristol Road to the new route. This was fairly simple to achieve as it mainly involved an agreement with J.P. Tudway and costs £300 6s.

Next they turned to something far more ambitious. In 1835-6 they acquired the properties on the west side of Wet Lane. They were demolished and the road was widened to create modern Broad Street (*38*). Its alignment was then continued across the fields to create a new direct route to Glastonbury, to be called Priory Road, as most of the route was on former hospital land. It in effect bypassed Southover although at the edge of town what was then the White Horse (later the Sherston Arms) survived by reversing its main entrance to its north side (*colour plate 28*).

Before the second scheme was under way the corporation also began to consider town improvement. This was a sign that it had recovered from the disputes of the 1820s. It returned to the question of marketing. There were good reasons to do so. In 1833 commissioners reported on all boroughs as a preliminary to reform. It described the town as at low ebb. The silk trade was wholly given up and the market for corn was down. In contrast the cheese market was the greatest in the West of England. One stocking factory remained and employed 150 people.

Little remained apart from the market function, so that needed cherishing. On 1 August 1834 the corporation resolved that a proper place be provided for 'exposing fish, butchers' meat, poultry and other provisions for sale'. The scheme took a definite form in early 1835 when the bishop expressed his willingness to sell two properties west of the palace and fronting Market Place (*36*). The corporation had to consider finance. Part of the loan from the Llewellyn

Almshouse Trustees was outstanding so attention turned to the town estate. It is striking that they and the bishop were now willing to sell their traditional estates. Presumably the prospect of reform which loomed over both made this more possible. The bishop had other reasons. Palace Mill was probably no longer viable as a grist mill and the experiment with silk production had failed. Also, as the corporation was to discover, it was ruinous.

The corporation was drawn into offering more and more property as the proposal developed but the end result was that, comparing 1834 and 1836, the number of freehold properties fell from 82 to 50 and the number of ground rents from nine to three. Income fell from £111 6s 5½d to £41 8s 6½d. The sales were conducted properly. Properties were valued by outside surveyors and on their advice a scheme for a general auction was abandoned. Instead properties were offered to the tenant. Only four tenants refused initially and in the end only one property went to auction. It alone did not reach its valuation. At £44 it was 15s short. At this stage there was only one objection. This was from William Henry Vowles, a schoolmaster and habitual complainer. Other 'highlights' of his career include being struck with a fish while acting as market bailiff and attending a vestry meeting with a placard of protest round his neck.

The transactions enable us to illustrate the relative positions of the freeholder and the tenant with a three-life lease. The corporation sold a Wet Lane property to Thomas Young who held it on a lease of 1831 for £69 18s. The next year Young sold it to the turnpike trust with vacant possession for £395. Similarly, the corporation paid the bishop £488 18s for the freehold of his two properties while the leaseholder, Archdeacon Henry Law, received £750. The actual occupiers were given respectively £25 and £10 to quit.

The corporation considered six tenders and selected the lowest from the local builder Richard George. The original intention was to keep modern 12 Market Place which was to serve as offices for the new market hall. The hall would be built on the sites of two lesser houses forming part of the same leasehold, and the gardens of these properties and that on the north of Palace Mill. The Mill itself was not affected. Now a series of extensions, problems and overruns began. We are now well aware that these tend to go with major projects. The corporation immediately added £25 to the price for a red deal roof. Then they had a report on Palace Mill. Inspection had shown it to be so dilapidated as to be beyond repair. Moreover, if it stood a further winter no reusable timbers would remain. It was a detriment to the new hall but offered potential. For £250 it could be removed and the site used for a cheese hall and parking for 150 carts. This would remove the cheese sales under the town hall and cure congestion in the market.

The proposal was approved and the corporation found itself in a rush to finish the project by Christmas and to raise more funds. By 23 November the cost of the cheese hall had crept up to £300. In December opposition surfaced. An application was made to the Vice-chancellor's court for injunctions against the corporation and Stuckey's Bank. These would have halted building and frozen funds. The application was on behalf of a citizen, Cornelius Bartlett. The Vice-chancellor was not impressed, asking how the information for the allegations was obtained and why action was started now when the project had been underway since June. He adjourned the hearing for a week to allow for full representation. The old corporation ended its days by having to meet on Christmas Eve, Christmas Day and Boxing Day in case of news from London.

In fact the action was never resumed. Partly, this was because of the election to the reformed council. On 30 December Robert Davies, the town clerk, wrote with a total lack of modern officer impartiality informing their London agents 'our election have ended beyond our expectations propitious. Eleven out of twelve of our list have been elected and the twelfth is decidedly in favour of the new market'. In any case the application was unlikely to succeed. It was riddled with factual errors. Many allegations were obvious false for example that none of the town estate had been sold before June 1835.

However, the hall was not finished in time. On 1 January 1836 the new council voted in its favour and established a committee to oversee completion and outstanding finance. The second, which included collecting legal costs from Bartlett, took some time complicated by the changed style and nature of the authority and the split of money between old and new treasurers (Scrase 1988).

The reformed council was able to wall in the ground floor of the town hall and extend its accommodation (39). Then in 1839 they were able to effect a final tidying of the area around the town hall. The 1779 sale of the town hall site had not included the Crown Inn and its neighbours. These remained as a perquisite for the archdeacon of Wells. In 1837 Archdeacon Law and the bishop sold the easternmost house, which protrudes in front of the town hall, to Joseph Lovell Lovell (whose repetitive name resulted from a name change from Joseph Lovell Teck in 1803 when he inherited from his mother's cousin Joseph Lovell). In 1839 Lovell sold the house and 18 and 20 High Street to the town for £1,460. The Treasury refused to sanction more property sales. Instead Lovell granted them a mortgage for £1,700 on the High Street properties and the shambles behind them to cover these and other costs. The corporation then removed the Market Place house to produce a more rectangular space in front of the town hall (36 and 37).

Meanwhile another of the reforms of the 1830s had been put into effect. A law of 1834 had transformed provision for the poor. The old system of parish-based relief in the home was swept away. Instead unions of parishes were to build workhouses. The Wells Union Workhouse was opened in 1837 on a site on Glastonbury Road. It was just beyond the edge of the then built-up area defined by the White Horse

39 The town hall as it was after the changes of 1835-6. The ground floor (previously open and used for the cheese market) has been walled in. The hall stood in this form for about 90 years until structural problems led to alterations. The balcony and high level circular windows (see *colour plate 19*) were added at that time

(41). This was the first extension of the built up area in this direction. The cathedral authorities maintained their independence from the new union. The Liberty had its own miniature workhouse to the rear of 7 St Andrew Street.

One last trend of the decade needs to be noted. Architectural fashion was changing from the classical inspired Georgian, and the interest in the Gothic was growing. Inevitably this increased interest in Wells Cathedral and its surrounds. Engraved drawings began to appear from 1830 culminating in the Pugins, father and son, publication *Examples of Gothic Architecture* which used many examples from Wells. Visitors were attracted, initially a discerning few. It also sparked the enthusiasm for both 'restoration' and romantic ruins. Bishop George Henry Law (1824 45) embodied both trends. He employed Benjamin Ferrey to rebuild Joscelin's hall, the original core of the palace. He also had much of the roofless remains of Burnell's great hall demolished to create a romantic garden feature and picnic place.

WAITING FOR THE RAILWAY 1840-1859

In 1840 Parliament commissioned a report on the state of turnpike trusts, given the abolition of a statutory duty of labour on road repairs and the emerging competition of the railways. The Wells trust was given a satisfactory report. Its roads were said to be generally in good condition. It was to be a long time before they were to be exposed to railway competition. This was unfortunate, as the early availability of good railway connections was then one of the keys to economic success. The other was proximity to a coal field which the city also lacked. Wells was to languish. Its previous assets vanished. For example, the railways killed the London–Exeter and Bath–Exeter coaches which had previously called.

The new decade saw two new uses. The Church of England was split between Evangelicals and Tractarians but both sides agreed that an Oxbridge degree was no longer a sufficient foundation for ordination. As a result the Wells Theological College was founded in 1840. The bishop's son, James Law, offered the lease of the Rib and it became the headmaster's house. Otherwise the teaching and students fitted in. The vicars' library was used for teaching. Some students lived in the Close but others were further afield.

The second followed in 1847. It was the Somerset County Lunatic Asylum (later Mendip Hospital). It was built on a 14.5ha (36-acre) site no doubt deliberately detached from the built-up area of East Wells. The committee of visiting magistrates which commissioned it ordered a building of plain cheerful character to accommodate 300 patients. It was intended that many of them should cultivate parts of the grounds both as therapy and to save costs.

Population continued to grow but the rate slowed, compared to the first third of the century. This contrasts starkly with runaway urban growth elsewhere. No doubt this slower growth, and indeed a fall of nearly 250 for the In Parish in the decade 1861-71, reflected poor employment prospects. The brush factories were the main local source of employment. Many inhabitants of working-class areas had a long walk to work. In 1841 a considerable number of agricultural workers still lived in East Wells. Others were paper makers and had to trudge to and from Wookey Hole or Dulcote each day.

Where did the new population live? The town hardly expanded. It took many years for properties to spread the length of Priory Road (41). Similarly, there were only small ribbons of cottages creeping along Portway and Bath Road. Most of the growth was concentrated into the existing plots with extra houses on back gardens. In Southover and St Thomas Street it was particularly common to find a whole court laid out along a plot (40). It would be entered by a narrow opening or arch and the houses would take all access and light from that side, with blank walls facing the next plot. Provision for water and sanitation

40 Nineteenth-century Courts

was minimal. Similar, but slightly more salubrious schemes, could be found everywhere except the Liberty. For example, the corporation had not sold their property comprising 73 and 75 High Street in 1835. In their 1821 survey it was shown to comprise four tenements. When they next had their estate surveyed in 1848 it contained no less than nine (*colour plates 29* and *30*).

The new survey was occasioned by concerns that tenants had been adjusting boundaries without permission. This was so, but the plans also show a different form of disorderly development. The western end of High Street features a small set-back in the building line even today. In the past it was greater. Between 1821 and 1848 the tenant of council owned 80 had built a front extension onto public space, while persons opposite had fenced off small front gardens. Further east 55 had also moved forward at the expense of the street. The council did not think it had the prime responsibility. In September 1848 it was reported that the house at 55 was a nuisance and obstruction. It was to be set back but the corporation only agreed to contribute £35 towards a public subscription to finance this.

School facilities began to improve. In 1829 the Blue School moved to new premises at the western end of Chamberlain Street. Then in 1858 Peter Sherston gave the hospital site to the bishop for the proposed Central School.

The abundance of drinking places remained a problem. The number of traditional fully-fledged inns continued to decline but the Beer Act 1830 had relaxed licensing arrangements. As a result there was an explosion in the number of beer houses in the period 1837 to 1860. Many were very short-lived and places such as the Queen Adelaide, Rising Sun, Valiant Soldier and Waterloo Hero are only known from occasional references in directories or the town billeting book.

The town authorities did not turn to health issues until after mid-century. Meanwhile, they were receiving new duties from Parliament. A rate was raised to employ, equip and house a new police force. Also they were still concerned with marketing. In the 1840s they made further unsuccessful attempts to recover the livestock markets from Priddy and Binegar. But it was left to public subscription to help safeguard the town's other asset, the assizes. Previously, the judges had been lodged in various places such as the large houses of the Liberty or George Hamilton's mansion. In 1843 a permanent lodging was secured by buying 19 New Street and conveying it to trustees. J.P. Tudway's heir, Robert Charles Tudway, agreed to sell the site and donated £200. Subsequently, he was persuaded to stand for Parliament. In 1852 he was elected, reviving the family connection. It proved to be short-lived as he died young in 1855. Just before his death he had purchased Stoberry House with its park and Beryl Farm from John Davis Sherston for £10,887 14s. In 1861 Milton Lodge was bought as a dower house for his widow. The family now had three large houses on the north side of town.

The 1848 Public Health Act created new authorities in problem areas but also put responsibilities on existing boroughs. One obvious improvement was to remove cattle sales from the centre of town. The council voted to relocate the market away from the Queen's Arms yard in 1849. But nobody wanted such a neighbour. It was to prove a long quest. It was only in the period 1858-60 that they turned to something even more necessary to undertake, which was sewering the town. In 1858 they took the preliminary step of improving their finances. They sold a further 28 properties to reduce their mortgage debt. By the end of the next decade only six remained. In 1859 a large-scale ordnance survey plan was commissioned. This, still in the town hall, is the first comprehensive and accurate representation of the town. It and the associated list of owners and occupiers provide an excellent picture.

Meanwhile the railway had finally arrived. The first company to show an interest was the Somerset Central Railway, soon to be part of the Somerset and

Dorset Joint, but it hesitated while it considered routes east. As a result the East Somerset Railway was approached. It was then building a line from what was, at that time, the Great Western's Weymouth branch at Witham to Shepton Mallet. In 1856 an extension to Wells was agreed. This provoked the Somerset Central to push on. Their branch from Glastonbury arrived in 1859. The next section will explain how the town came to acquire two more stations.

THE LATE VICTORIAN PERIOD 1860-1901

The East Somerset line arrived in 1862 having breached the unity of the bishop's park and split the central wood into two. Its station was opposite that of the Somerset. and Dorset Joint Railway with Priory Road separating them. As the stations were peripheral the major inns, the Swan, the Star and the Mitre, bought coaches to ferry passengers to and from the train. On the strength of this link the Star was entered as the Star and Railway Hotel in the 1859 Directory. The Sherston Arms was better placed to benefit and was substantially improved in 1862 and renamed the Railway Hotel (*colour plate 28*). Similarly the nearest beerhouse became the Railway Tavern. It was 33 Southover and had been the Travellers Rest since 1839.

A third line arrived in 1870. This was a branch from the Bristol and Exeter line at Yatton which ran via Cheddar to a third station at Tucker Street. The Bristol and Exeter and East Somerset Railways each formed part of the Great Western. Rivalry between the GWR and S & DJR precluded co-operation at Wells. So for a time the termini each had their own engine sheds and turntables. Eventually in 1878 a level crossing was built at Priory Road. The GWR obtained running rights to use nine chains (594ft; 181m) of S & DJR track for which they paid £400 per annum. They then built a spur to Tucker Street (*41* and *42*). As a result they were able to work trains from Yatton to Witham and close their Priory Road station. Until 1934 their trains steamed slowly through their rival's station without stopping. This frightened generations of strangers but also precluded any advantage Wells might have gained as a minor junction.

Schools were evolving. By 1880 the Cathedral School was in difficulties with an aged master and premises. It was moved to the modern museum site and given a new head. In 1883 Chancellor Bernard provided the £1,500 to allow the conversion of Canons' Barn to classrooms. Wells Museum found its first home in part of the vacated accommodation over the west cloister. In 1885 the Blue School girls moved to new premises on Portway.

The other major physical change concerned the relocation of the livestock market. The council had to build a new road to site this unpopular neighbour.

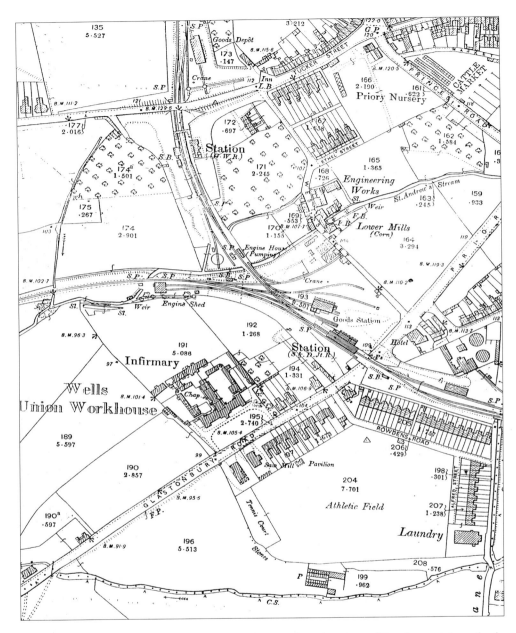

41 The western edge of Wells from the 1886 OS map. Perhaps the most striking feature is how slowly the town has grown. The western end of Priory Road is unbuilt after more than 40 years. Similarly Prince's Road serves only the cattle market. New by-law housing is limited to two groups around the surviving railway stations. By this time the East Somerset station had gone but its site is obvious on the east of Priory Road

42 The S & DJR spacious goods yard at Wells with their station and the level crossing to the right. The GWR spurs branches away crossing the yard to leave on the left. *Courtesy the Blencowe Collection*

In 1863 they bought parts of several gardens and orchards from the Sherstons and another paddock from the various heirs of James Baron. They then laid out Princes Road and sited the market between it and what then became Market Street. One other transaction of that year is worth mentioning as it saw Tudway holdings peak. Charles Clement Tideway entered into an exchange with the dean and chapter. He received the site of the canonical house at former 13 North Liberty. In return he surrendered the further of the two parcels behind Tower House and a parcel to the rear of 11. He used the site he gained to provide a conservatory for the Cedars.

The railways brought more visitors to the town, either specifically to it or by offering day trips from the new holiday resorts of the Somerset coast (*43*). Visits were encouraged by the continued interest in the Gothic. The antiquarian John Henry Parker produced his *Antiquities of the City of Wells* in 1866. The local photographer Thomas William Phillips was probably even more influential. In 1871 the front of the cathedral was scaffolded so that the statues could be inspected and secured. Phillips hauled his massive glass-plate camera up the ladders to photograph the statues and expanded the work into what amounted to a photographic survey of the cathedral (*44* and *45*). His work was much admired and widely disseminated. His letters of appreciation included one from John Ruskin.

43 Poster advertising a railway excursion to Wells (and Glastonbury). This example of 1876 was provided by the S & DJR for holidaymakers at Burnham-on-Sea

44 A typical example of Thomas Phillips' work at the cathedral. This is one of a set recording the carvings on the misericords of the choir

Some restoration was inevitable. Luckily the architects concerned with the cathedral lacked the heavy hand and view that they knew best which characterised most of their contemporaries. The cathedral was repaired rather than remodelled. In addition, Parker restored one of the houses on Vicars' Close, removing the then prevalent Georgian windows and doors. The various almshouse structures were ageing and this, rather than architectural fashion, necessitated attention. The council were shocked to find that the agreement of 1436 made them responsible for Bubwith's Almshouse. However, the more dramatic changes were to Llewellyn's Almshouse which was totally rebuilt on an enlarged site incorporating three further properties adjoining the original range and a strip of garden to the east. The new group incorporated Charles Almshouse.

It had long been the custom for the clergy of the diocese to study its history and that of the cathedral. It is a tradition that runs on from Giso's autobiographic fragment incorporated into the *Historiola* to Canon Bailey's studies of the properties in the Liberty of the late twentieth century. But now new fields began to open up. The town clerk Thomas Serel began to work on the vast archives of the town authority. He published relatively little but also gave a series of important lectures and left a mass of notes. The first archaeological excavation followed when in 1894 Edmund Buckle investigated the site of the two successive Lady chapels in the cloisters.

45 A further example showing a column capital carved with a fox escaping with a goose. A man looks on, his stone and cudgel useless

The other characteristic of this period is of attempts to correct inherited problems. Partly, this comes out of central initiatives in the period from the great Public Health Act of 1875 to the Local Government Act 1894. In part it came from voluntary activity, notably a lively temperance movement which was to institute a vigorous attack on the numerous drinking places in Wells.

Beginning with public reforms, there were two conflicting pressures. Wells was losing traditional rights but the reformed council was also having new duties placed on it. Already in 1866 separate civil parishes were created for St Cuthbert's In, St Cuthbert's Out and St Andrew's. Then, in 1867, the city had lost its right to return two MPs. It now shared one with a wider constituency. Subsequently in 1875 the council had its public health duties widened. It was required to produce building by-laws and to approve (or refuse) proposals in accordance with these. From the 1850s there had been optional powers to provide working-class housing and to close or clear unhealthy slums. These had never been used. Unpleasant as the courts of Southover and East Wells were, the medical officer of health was unwilling to recommend closure in the absence of alternative accommodation. He had no wish to force people into the workhouse. Then in 1890 these housing powers became a duty. In 1894 the County Council was established. It took over many administrative functions previously undertaken by the magistrates. Initially its offices were spread around the county and Wells gained as it, for some time, shared the council meetings with Taunton. But over the following 80 years the county council was to increasingly take over strategic functions such as roads and education from the boroughs and districts.

The temperance movement got underway in the 1870s. It was always fragmented. The Church of England and the various nonconformist groups all had their own temperance societies supplemented by bands of hope for the young. Indeed, the Church of England came to have separate organisations for St Cuthbert's and St Thomas'. As regards the later, this was a new church to serve East Wells, consecrated in 1857. It was part of a wider movement to provide more churches and chapels. A further chapel had been provided in Union Street, sometime after 1821 but certainly present by 1835, and the theatre became another by 1845. Then, in 1874, the Catholic Church bought the former Hamilton mansion in Chamberlain Street. Subsequently a new church was provided on part of the gardens (over the site of Moniers Lane). The house became a convent and the former stables on Union Street a school. Victorian religious enthusiasm was at its height.

Building on this religious fervour the temperance movement made rapid headway. Its lectures, other publicity and sponsorship of the 'pledge' (not to drink) hit the trade hard. A Licensed Victuallers Protection Association was formed in 1887 to counter these pressures. But the campaign was also more direct. Inns were bought up. In 1888 Mary Cox acquired the Old City Brewery and conveyed it to the trustees of the Theological College. This enabled Buckle to undertake its restoration in the more usual Victorian sense of a substantial rebuild (*colour plate 23*). It then became the college library (and subsequently Wells Cathedral School's music school). Later the Mitre was closed and the Red Lion converted to a temperance hotel and coffee room for over 20 years. Others such as the Central Coffee Tavern next to the King's Head in High Street and the St Thomas Street Coffee Tavern did less well. Other inns were falling victim to more general economic pressures. Thus the George was replaced by a new building for Stuckey's Bank.

NEW CENTURY 1901–1918

The new century brought no dramatic changes. In fact one change that was to transform the employment structure for most of the twentieth century must have seemed very minor initially. In 1900 Alma James Clare arrived from Norfolk to open a drapers shop at 4 High Street. He soon became the partner of John Holloway who ran a large general store occupying several of the New Works. They sold groceries, provisions, clothes and furniture. Five years later the energetic Clare was sole proprietor and was opening branches in villages in

46 An early motor coach excursion about to leave Market Place shortly before the First World War. The ladies waiting to board wear the heavy coats, hats and veils then thought necessary for such travel. Note also the Clare name on the New Works and the total absence of crenellations on the turrets of the Bishop's Eye and the two houses adjoining it in contrast with later views

the area (*46*). He also became interested in the potential offered by the farming community. In a room over the shop he began to make cheese cloths and milk filters. These ideas were to bear fruit after 1919.

This was the period when the young Elizabeth Goudge lived in Wells and it is portrayed in her novel *A City of Bells* and later in her autobiography *The Joy of Snow*. These show how grim St Thomas Street still was, despite public heath reforms and the decrease in numbers of inns and beerhouses.

A link with some 150 years of history was broken in 1909 when the Tudways had to give up living in the Cedars and retire to Milton Lodge. They could not find a tenant for the house immediately.

The First World War had inevitable impacts in the disappearance of young men into the army, shortages and then rationing. Also Lloyd George's tightening of the licensing laws (although intended to stop drinking by munitions and shipyard workers) had the effect of closing yet more drinking houses. Losses included the (third) King's Arms in St John Street and the Butcher's Arms in

47 The Red Cross Hospital in the Cedars in the First World War. Tudway family portraits still look down on the soldiers and nurses

High Street. But the citizens were probably most directly exposed to the effects of modern war by the opening of a Red Cross hospital in the Cedars (47).

SUMMING UP: A PERIOD OF MAJOR CHANGE

Over the period covered in this chapter much had been transformed. The franchise had been altered and the corporation reformed. Burgess status no longer mattered and the resident gentry, who had played a major role in town affairs since the sixteenth century, had vanished. The town had lost its textile industries after six centuries. The traditional estates had been dispersed and property ownership was more fragmented than it had been since 1325. The railway had arrived but late and in the form of minor lines.

However, in two respects it remained little changed. The cathedral continued and it was still a small market town (48). It had grown by under 500 persons in this period compared with over 15,000 at Weston-Super-Mare. As a result, physical expansion was slight. It took over 50 years before Priory Road was fully built up. Ribbons had crept along Portway, Burcott Road (formerly the western end of Tucker Street but separately named after the railway split that road), North

48 May Market, 1897. This Phillips' picture shows the continuing vitality of the market. The portion of sign on the right shows that the Red Lion was now a temperance hotel. Note the two properties on the left now replaced with a single-storey bank. They have been given a more modern Georgian front at some time since they were portrayed in *36*

Road and Bath Road. Much of the development was of a low-priced cottage type, but by the Edwardian period substantial semi-detached villas' aimed at the middle class were appearing on Portway. Similarly one of four new streets, Portway Avenue, was aimed at this market. The others, Ethel Street, Rowden Road and Alfred Street (the last two part of a single scheme), were lined by standard by-law terrace houses. These were only started late in this period. For example, the Ecclesiastical Commissioners did not breach the bounds of the bishop's park by selling Rowden Close until 1885. These by-law houses were aimed at the lower middle class or skilled workers, in other words clerks, senior shop assistants, foremen and skilled artisans. The less fortunate remained in the courts of Southover and East Wells.

11

A PLEASANT PLACE TO BE
1919–2000

In the last 80 years Wells has witnessed unparalleled growth in physical extent and population. One key reason was the lack of economic success in the previous period. As a result the physical fabric had not been transformed. Much survived from Bekynton's time and a large amount of housing appeared to be Georgian. This and a picturesque setting (*colour plate 1*) made the city ever more attractive as a place to visit or to live. The development of road transport made both tourism and commuting easier. After about 1960 road transport and telecommunications also freed industry and offices from many traditional geographical constraints. Firms could locate to areas where they might attract skilled workers or where their executives could enjoy a suitable lifestyle. Employment prospects improved, fuelling further population growth.

BETWEEN THE WARS

Immediately after the First World War the Cedars found a new use. There was a backlog of candidates for ordination so it was leased by the Theological College. By 1925 this problem had been dealt with and the cathedral school was able to take over the lease. In the previous year it had just 24 pupils. It now stood on the verge of its great expansion. However, it abandoned its house on Cathedral

Green which was sold to the museum trustees. Nevertheless, it had expanded to over 100 boys by 1934 when the Church Commissioners bought 23 East Liberty for it.

As life returned to normal in the 1920s growth became the dominant trend. This was apparent in both housing and industrial structure. The first council houses were built and there were a growing number of new privately-built houses. Many were substantial, catering for the more affluent, including commuters and the retired who found Wells an attractive place to settle. But the more dramatic changes were in industry, thanks to the enterprise of A.J. Clare. He expanded his range of dairy-orientated products from cheese cloths and filters to milk filters, overalls for dairy staff and products for cleaning the dairy. Soon he could supply milking stools, covered buckets, coolers and a variety of brushes and brooms. Initially he went from farm to farm persuading farmers of the importance of dairy hygiene.

Clare began to buy up firms which could contribute to this range. As early as 1921 the 70 year-old local paper, the *Wells Journal*, was acquired as A.J. Clare saw the potential of printing for the business side of dairying. Hilliers followed in 1927 to provide stools and brushes. By 1939 Ditcheat Weaving and Frank Bryan and Paton had followed. The former provided cheese cloths and bandages while the latter made scientific instruments. Clare's enterprises and acquisitions progressively took over the space behind the town hall where the former New Works gardens and Slovens Acre became a manufacturing zone.

All this helped to diversify the employment structure. In addition, increasing numbers of visitors by bicycles, cars and motor coaches help to keep the shops viable and led to the appearance of several new cafes. As a result, what were often two depressed decades elsewhere were relatively prosperous in Wells. The signs of change must have been confirmed for the poor when national reforms abolished the workhouse. The building was converted to a hospital.

By 1933 the demand for new housing was sufficient to result in a major boundary review. The area of the city was nearly doubled with 250 hectares (617 acres) added to a pre-existing 291 hectares (719 acres). At the same time the former civil parishes of St Andrew and St Cuthbert In were merged to give a single civil parish of Wells.

THE SECOND WORLD WAR

The War was experienced indirectly in Wells. It was never attacked, missing the so-called Baedeker raids which hit Bath and many cathedral cities. This, of course, was unknown at the time and the Levels were seen as suitable landings for paratroops and gliders. As a result, the anti-tank trench mentioned earlier was dug across the park and other relics of a defensive line in the form of concrete blocks ('dragons teeth') and pill boxes can still be found in the surrounding countryside.

Wells had all the usual experiences of conscription, shortages and rationing plus the many campaigns for savings, collecting salvage and digging for victory. It also received a large number of evacuees from more threatened locations. These reached 850 in August 1941 and there were the usual social problems as a result. However, Wells also received whole schools. Brandon Girls School moved from Bristol and was accommodated in parts of the palace, deanery and other Church-owned properties. Normanton, a boys preparatory school, came from Bexhill. The death of Prebendary Dennison meant that they were accommodated at 19 East Liberty while their teaching was integrated with the cathedral school. After the War the school retained this additional building. Wells relatively remote location also saw some additional industry relocated. There were some very different arrivals. Prisoner-of-war camps were established around the city at Penleigh, Stoberry and Maesbury. They accommodated both German and Italian prisoners who were mainly put to work on local farms.

DEPARTURES, MOVES AND ARRIVALS 1946–75

After the War a period of a quarter of a century saw the loss of many features which had characterised the town since at least 1800. Some were not to be regretted. For example, the council now launched a campaign which closed the majority of the courts of Southover and St Thomas Street. One grander house also vanished – Stoberry House was demolished. A final rationalisation of Tudway holdings followed in 1967 when the freehold of the Cedars was sold to the dean and chapter. Milton Lodge was retained as the family's local base. By the end of the '60s the railways had gone.

By the 1950s it was apparent that the canonical houses were no longer appropriate for their purpose. Canons could no longer afford their upkeep which was becoming more exacting with the listing of historic buildings. Also, they usually lacked the extensive families to fill them and could not afford the servants to staff them. In 1953 Dean Woodforde, a widower, declined to live in the deanery. He was accommodated in Vicars' Close and the Diocesan Board of Finance moved in with a grant of £500 for necessary repairs. A further major reorganisation was undertaken by 1970. Four new canonical houses were built in the rear garden of the deanery, which was now renamed 'The Old Deanery'. In addition 25 East Liberty had been refurbished and Dean Edwards moved in to what became 'The Dean's Lodgings'. The former canonical houses became parts of the cathedral school. This was well timed as it had just been recognised as a specialist music school and had become co-educational. In contrast, the demand for education for Anglican clergy was declining. In 1971 Wells Theological College was merged with that at Salisbury and relocated there. A further series of buildings passed to the school which became the dominant use in the northern section of the Liberty. In 1970 the Blue School was also reorganised, being merged with the secondary school to form a new comprehensive.

Just prior to the loss of the college, Wells had lost two other established if very different features. In 1967 Hilliers closed in the face of cheap imports. Then in 1970 the assizes were consolidated at Taunton. But the loss that was felt most followed in 1974. Local government reform took away most of the powers of the town authority. The new Mendip District Council took over responsibility for such matters as housing and public health. There was still a Wells City Council but its powers were basically those of a rural parish. It took the city over 200 years to achieve self-government, now after nearly 400 years these were gone.

All these losses had been balanced by accelerating residential expansion and continued industrial development. As regards the former, Wells had a population of 5,835 at the 1951 census. Initially post-war austerity and shortages checked expansion. Between 1951 and 1961 growth averaged 1.4 per cent a year. In the decade 1961-71 it increased to 2.5 per cent. In 1971, just prior to the change of status, population was 8,604.

Turning to industry, Clares expanded by a number of subsidiary firms. Sutherland Thompson was a wholesale firm supplying laboratory equipment, initially for dairying but expanding to deal with industry, educational establishments and government. Clariloid Chemicals manufactured paints and fungicides to counter rust and moulds. In addition EMI took over the electrics factory which had arrived during the War. It built up the business to eventually specialise in scanners and government contracts. This growth was still restricted by Mendip to the north and the bishop's park on the south. Industrial development did encroach on the western fringe of the park adjoining Southover and Glastonbury Road but otherwise it survived. The result was an increasing east–west extent to the built-up area.

FURTHER GROWTH AND TRAFFIC PROBLEMS 1975–2000

A number of factors brought the question of traffic to the fore. The growth of Wells increased movements around the town. Partly, it was, of course, the build-up of vehicles and journeys in national terms. There were also local elements. The building boom boosted the Mendip quarries and this meant that many of their lorries traversed the town. As the main roads converged on the town centre much of this traffic passed along High Street. This made Wells less pleasant for shoppers and tourists. Inevitably the county, as highway authority, produced schemes for relief roads bypassing the centre. The first scheme used the old railway tracks on the west, then followed the rear of Chamberlain Street before turning north to the top of New Street, then skirting Stoberry Park and threading its way through East Wells until it eventually reached the head of Tor Street and the road to Shepton Mallet. This eastern section involved the loss of houses. It succeeded at the planning stage but fell when the compulsory purchase orders were contested. A modified scheme abandoned the eastern section, continuing along the rear of Chamberlain Street to link up with Montery Road (previously extending west only to Milton Lane). Traffic heading towards Shepton Mallet from the north now has to loop around the town centre to join a new road following the railway alignment across the park.

The implementation of this second scheme allowed improvements to the pedestrian realm in the centre. There was also extensive re-paving and the removal of unattractive road signs and double yellow lines (*colour plates 18 and 19*). The centre became more pleasant but other areas paid, with extra traffic passing their houses. The works did not provide every answer. Parking is short, particularly close to the cathedral. There have been suggestions for car parks on both Tor Furlong and the Bishop's Camery. Both would impinge on the striking rural approach to the cathedral along the old road from Shepton Mallet and, to date, they have been rejected.

Repaving has also been a feature of the extensive works undertaken in and around the cathedral. However, the earliest and most ambitious campaign involved the restoration of the West Front. This was launched in October 1976 with a national appeal for £1,300,000. The resultant works included experiments as to the best methods of protection and involved undoing many unforeseen consequences of Victorian restoration. This phase culminated in the placing of three modern statues in the top-most gable. Previously this area had contained the lower half of a Christ flanked by two empty niches. Now there is a modern Christ paid for by the Friends of Wells Cathedral flanked by two seraphim financed by the dean and the chapter. Since that time works have continued around the cathedral and more is to come in the form of a visitor centre with a restaurant relocated from the west cloister. All this activity has given Dr Warwick Rodwell many opportunities to study the fabric. The results of the earlier stages are written up in his two volume Wells Cathedral: excavations and structural studies 1978–83 (*colour plates 5 and 6*).

1801		1901		2001	
1. Bath	28,768	1. Bath	46,644	1. Bath	90,144
2. Frome	8,748	2. Taunton	19,535	2. Weston-super-Mare	80,076
3. Taunton	5,794	3. Weston-super-Mare	18,275	3. Taunton	58,241
4. Shepton Mallet	5,104	4. Bridgwater	13,639	4. Yeovil	41,871
5. Wellington	4,033	5. Frome	11,828	5. Bridgwater	36,563
6. Bridgwater	3,634	6. Yeovil	11,704	6. Frome	24,171
7. Chard	2,784	7. Norton-Radstock	9,155	7. Clevedon	21,957
8. Yeovil	2,774	8. Wellington	7,283	8. Burnham	21,476
9. Crewkerne	2,576	9. Chard	6,318	9. Norton-Radstock	20,049
10. Wells	2,497	10. Clevedon	5,900	10. Nailsea	17,649
		11. Shepton Mallet	5,446	11. Portishead	17,130
		12. Crewkerne	5,172	12. Keynsham	15,533
		13. Burnham	4,922	13. Chard	12,008
		14. Glastonbury	4,141	14. Minehead	11,699
		15. Wells	4,063	15. Street	11,669
				16. Wellington	10,599
				17. Wells	10,406

49 Wells and the larger towns of Somerset 1801-2001

While these events have provided most controversy growth has continued. The closure of Mendip Hospital and the residential development of its site means that Wells is now 4km (2½ miles) east–west compared with the 1.7km (1 mile) of the medieval and early modern town. In contrast, the continued barriers of Mendip on one side and the park and Tor Hill on the other mean that it is still restricted north–south. The pre-modern town was at maximum 640m (700 yds) wide and generally 550m (600 yds) or less. In places it is still 640m wide although more commonly 915m (1,000 yds). It is only in the extreme west, beyond the park that it increases to 1.8km. The development of the Hospital site has pushed the built up area beyond the limits of 1933. They are also exceeded at the Racal factory. Residential growth has led to changes in school provision. The Central School has moved to a new site and its former location has been used for houses. By the 2001 census the population had reached 10,406.

Industry has expanded and changed. The switches in demand and technology plus the processes of take-over and merger have transformed the scene. The once ubiquitous Clare name is seen less. Again the industrial zone behind the town hall has gone, replaced by housing. Most of the industry is now in large easily accessible premises on the Glastonbury Road. However, the massive cheese factory and store there show continuity with long traditions. The expansion of employment is such that Wells now receives a net inward flow of commuters although movement northwards to Bath and Bristol continues.

There have been other changes. The number of inns continues to fall. The Star has vanished after nearly 500 years. But other eating-places multiply. For example, when the main post office closed part became a pizza restaurant. Also, some court functions have returned to Wells as a result of problems at Taunton.

The latest planning proposals recognised site restraints and proposed only limited growth. New housing is to be on former industrial sites, the former Mendip Foods factory and Priory Mills (already completed at the time of writing). New industry is to be accommodated on a site adjoining Gate Lane and the new road to Shepton. Additional parking is proposed by Palace Farm. These last two involve further encroachment on the northwest fringe of the park.

So the population of Wells has grown 2½ times since 1901 and is four times larger than it was when the town was at its most significant in the national hierarchy. Nevertheless, it remains a small place in relative terms as other towns have grown faster. It was the tenth town in Somerset in 1801, had fallen to fifteenth by 1901 and is now seventeenth. Although it has passed Crewkerne, Shepton Mallet and Glastonbury, that had overtaken it in the period 1750-1900, it has been exceeded by many new creations (49). Most are coastal resorts or commuting settlements around Bristol but also include nearby Street. Wells still relies to a marked extent on the cathedral, an advantageous site and the services it provides for the surrounding area. In this sense its prosperity is a sign of continuity.

BIBLIOGRAPHY

Bailey D.S. 1982 *Canonical Houses of Wells* Alan Sutton, Gloucestershire

—, 1985 *Wells Manor of Canon Grange* Alan Sutton, Gloucestershire

Britnell R.H. 1986 *Growth and Decline in Colchester* Cambridge University Press

Boone M. and Stabel P. (eds) 2000 *Shaping Urban Identity in Late Medieval Europe* Garant, Leuven and Apeldoorn

Borsay P. 1989 *The English Urban Renaissance* Clarendon Press, Oxford

Bush R.J. 1975 *The Book of Taunton* Barracuda, London

Carus-Wilson E.M. (ed.) 1937 *The Overseas Trade of Bristol in the Later Middle Ages* Bristol Record Society (Vol. 7), Bristol

Chandler J. (ed.) 1993 *John Leland's Itinerary* Alan Sutton, Stroud

Colchester L.S. 1984 *Wells Cathedral Communar's Accounts 1327-1600* Friends of Wells Cathedral, Wells

—, 1987 *Wells Cathedral* Unwin Hyman, London

—, 1988 *Wells Cathedral Escheator's Accounts 1369-1600* Privately, Wells

Colchester L.S., Tudway Quilter D.C. and Quilter A. 1985 *A History of Wells Cathedral School* Wells Cathedral School

Collinson J. 1791 *The History and Antiquities of the County of Somerset* 3 vols., Cruttwell, Bath

Defoe D. 1948 *A Tour Through England and Wales* 2 vols. Everyman, London

Dickinson F.H. (ed.) 1889 *Kirkby's Quest for Somerset, etc* SRS (vol. 3), Taunton

Dunning R.W. 1983 *A History of Somerset* (2nd edition) Phillimore, Chichester

Dyer A. 1991 *Decline and Growth in English Towns 1400-1640* Macmillan, London

—, 2000 'Ranking Lists of English Medieval Towns' in Palliser (2000) 747-70

Eliassen F.E. and Erslund G.A. (eds) 1996 *Power, Profit and Urban Land* Scolar, Aldershot.

Everitt A. 1967 'The Marketing of Agricultural Produce' *Agrarian History of England and Wales Vol. 4 1500-1640* Cambridge University Press, 466-592

Green E. (ed.) 1888 *Colleges, Chantries, etc in Somerset in 1548* SRS (Vol. 2), Taunton

—, 1904 *Certificates of Muster 1569* SRS (Vol. 20), Taunton

Harris R. 2002 'Political Arithmetic: the census in St Thomas Street 1841 to 1891' *History round Wells* 6, 3-16

Hasler J. 2002 'Queen Anne's Visit to Wells' *History round Wells* 5, 21-3

Hobhouse E. (ed.) 1887 *Register of John de Drokensford, Bishop of Bath and Wells, 1309-29* SRS (vol. 1), Taunton

—, (ed.) 1934 *The Diary of a West Country Physician 1684-1726* Simpkin Marshall, London

Holmes T.S. (ed.) 1896 *Register of Ralph of Shrewsbury* 2 vols. SRS (vols. 9-10), Taunton

—, (ed.) 1899 *Register of Walter Giffard, Bishop of Bath and Wells, 1265-6, and of Henry Bowett, 1401-7* SRS (vol. 13), Taunton

—, 1908 *Wells and Glastonbury* Methuen, London

—, (ed.) 1914 *Register of Nicholas Bubwith, Bishop of Bath and Wells* 2 vols. SRS (vols. 29-30), Taunton

—, (ed.) 1915-16 *Register of John Stafford, Bishop of Bath and Wells* 2 vols. SRS (vols. 31-2), Taunton

Hooper L. 1995 'Evacuees' *Report WNHAS* 107, 4-11

—, 2000 'The Demon Drink: the temperance movement in Wells 1870-1900' *History round Wells* 1, 17-31

Hunter J. (ed.) 1840 *Historiola de Primordiis Episcopatus Somersetensis: Ecclesiastical Documents* Camden Society (1st series 3), London

Johnson R. 2002 'Wells and the Monmouth Rebellion' *History round Wells* 5, 3-10

Judd A.F. 1961 *The life of Thomas Bekynton* Phillimore, Chichester

Keene D. 1985 *Survey of Medieval Winchester* 2 vols. Clarendon Press, Oxford

Kelly P. 2003 'Wells Theological College' *History round Wells* 7, 23-36

Kowaleski M. 1995 *Local Markets and Regional Trade in Medieval Exeter.* Cambridge University Press

Maxwell-Lyte C. (ed.) 1937 *Registers of Robert Stillington 1466-91 and Richard Fox, 1492-4* SRS (vol. 52), Taunton

—, (ed.) 1939 *Registers of Oliver King and Hadrian de Castello* SRS (vol. 54), Taunton

—, (ed.) 1940 *Bishops Registers 1518-1559* SRS (vol. 55), Taunton

Maxwell-Lyte C. and Dawes M.C.B. (eds) 1934-5 *Register of Thomas Bekynton, Bishop of Bath and Wells, 1443-65* 2 vols. SRS (vols. 49-50), Taunton

Mead M. 1980 *The Book of Wells* Barracuda, Nottingham

Morris C. (ed.) 1949 *The Journeys of Celia Fiennes* Cresset Press, London

Neale F. 2003/4 'The Old Deanery Garden I' *Report WNHAS* 115, 3-9

Nott A. 2001 'Poxe, Puncke and Puritane' *History round Wells* 4, 2-40

—, 2002 'Domesday Book: the Wells entry' *History round Wells* 6, 18-34

Nott A. and Hasler J. (eds) 2004 *Wells Convocation Act Books 1589-1665* 2 vols. SRS (vols. 90 and 91), Taunton

Palliser D.M. 1979 *Tudor York* Oxford University Press

—, 2000 *Cambridge Urban History of Britain I 600-1540* Cambridge University Press

Palmer T.F. (ed.) 1924 *Collectanea I* SRS (vol. 39), Taunton

Peacock C. 2000 'Wells Borough Boundaries' *History round Wells* 2, 2-19

Pevsner N. 1958 *The Buildings of England: North Somerset and Bristol* Penguin, Harmondsworth

Pooley C. 1877 *The Old Stone Crosses of Somerset* Longmans Green, London

Reid R. and Scrase A.J. 1981 'A great house and two lost lanes at Wells' *Proceedings SANHS* 125, 32-43

Robinson A.E. (ed) 1922 *The life of Richard Kidder* SRS (vol. 37), Taunton

Rodwell W. 2001 *Wells Cathedral: excavations and structural studies 1978-83* English Heritage, London

Scrase A.J. 1982a 'The mills at Wells' *Notes and Queries for Somerset and Dorset* xxxi 238-43

—, 1982b 'The Medieval Chapel at Southover in Well' *Proceedings SANHS* 126, 107-10

—, 1983 'Wells High Street: continuity and change' *Report WNHAS* 95 & 6, 5-12

—, 1984 'Wells Inns' *Notes and Queries for Somerset and Dorset* xxxi 378-95

—, 1987 'Wells Inns' *Notes and Queries for Somerset and Dorset* xxxii 573-76

—, 1988 'Municipal Reform, Wells Corporation and its estates' *Southern History* 10, 129-41

—, 1989a 'A French Merchant in Fourteenth Century Wells' *Proceedings SANHS* 133, 131-40

—, 1989b 'Development and Change in Burgage Plots: the example of Wells' *Journal of Historical Geography* 15(4), 349-65

—, 1989c *Wells: a study of town origins and early development* UWE, Bristol

—, 1989d 'Wells Almshouse records and topographic reconstruction at Wells' *Notes and Queries for Somerset and Dorset* xxxii, 738-48

—, 1989/90 'What's in a name – the inhabitants of Wells c.1215-1350' *Report WNHAS* 101 & 2, 26-40

—, 1992 *Wells: a Pictorial History* Phillimore, Chichester

—, 1993 *Wells: the anatomy of a medieval and early modern property market* UWE, Bristol

—, 1996 'Working with British Property Records: the Potential and the Problems' in Eliassen and Erslund (1996) 15-38

—, 1999 *Streets and Market Places in Southwest England: encroachments and improvements* Edwin Mellen Press, Lampeter

—, 2000 'Crosses, conduits and other street furniture in the south west of England' in Boone and Stabel (2001) 201-19

—, 2002a 'The citizens of medieval Wells' *History round Wells* 6, 35-46

—, 2002b *Medieval Town Planning: a modern invention?* UWE, Bristol

— 2003a 'The inhabitants of Wells 1600-1649' *History round Wells* 7, 3-22

—, 2003b The urban estate of Bubwith's Almshouse, Wells *Notes and Queries for Somerset and Dorset* xxxv, 216-227

—, 2005a 'The 1524 Lay Subsidy at Wells' *History round Wells* 9, 15-45

—, 2005b *Somerset Towns: changing fortunes 800-1800* Tempus, Stroud

Scrase A.J. and Dunning R.W. 'The Bishop's Palace Wells' *Notes and Queries for Somerset and Dorset* xxxv, 52-5 (Eds)

Scrase A.J. and Hasler J. 2002 *Wells Corporation Properties* SRS (Vol. 87), Taunton

Shaw D.G. 1993 *The Creation of a Community* Clarendon Press, Oxford

Shilton D. and Holsworthy R. (eds) 1932 *Wells City Charters* SRS (Vol. 46), Taunton

Stanton W.I. 1987/88 'The ancient springs, streams and underground watercourses of the City of Wells' *Report WNHAS* 100, 25-48

Stokes J. 1985-6 'The Wells Cordwainers Show' *Comparative Drama* 19(4), 332-44

Stokes J. and Alexander R.J. (eds) 1996 *Records of Early English Drama: Somerset* 2 vols. Toronto University Press

Tudway Quilter D.C. 1985 'The Cedars and the Tudways' in Colchester, Tudway Quilter and Quilter 58-103

Underdown D. 1963 'A case concerning bishop's land: Cornelius Burges and the corporation of Wells' *English Historical Review* New Series 78, 18-48

—, 1973 *Somerset in the Civil War and Interregnum* David and Charles, Newton Abbot

Weaver F.W. (ed.) 1901 *Somerset Medieval Wills (1383-1500)* SRS (Vol. 16), Taunton

—, 1903 *Somerset Medieval Wills (1500-1530)* SRS (Vol. 19), Taunton

—, 1905 *Somerset Medieval Wills (1531-1558)* SRS (Vol. 21), Taunton

Webb A.J. (ed.) 2002 *Two Tudor Subsidy Assessments for the County of Somerset 1558 and 1581-2* SRS (Vol. 88), Taunton

APPENDIX – DIOCESAN BISHOPS

BISHOPS OF WELLS

Athelm 909-23
Wulfhelm I 923-6
Aelfeah 926-37
Wulfhelm II 938-55
Brithelm 956-74
Cyneward 974-5
Sigar 975-997
Aelfwine 997-99
Lyfing 999-1013
Aethelwine 1013-23
Brihtwig alias Merewit 1024-33
Dudoc 1033-60
Giso 1061-88

BISHOPS OF BATH

John of Tours (or de Villula) 1088-1122
Godfrey 1123-35
Robert of Lewes 1136-66
Reginald de Bohun (or Fitzjocelin) 1174-91

BISHOPS OF BATH AND GLASTONBURY

Savaric Fitzgeldewin 1192-1205
Joscelin of Wells (or Trotman) 1206-42
(Bishop of Bath only from 1219)

BISHOPS OF BATH AND WELLS

Roger of Salisbury 1244-7
William Bytton I 1248-64
Walter Giffard 1265-6
William Bytton II 1267-74
Robert Burnell 1275-92
William of March 1293-1302
Walter Haselshaw 1302-8
John Droxensford 1309-29
Ralph of Shrewsbury 1329-63
John Barnet 1363-6
John Harewell 1367-86
Walter Skirlaw 1386-8

Ralph Ergum 1386-1400
Henry Bowet 1401-7
Nicholas Bubwith 1407-24
John Stafford 1425-43
Thomas Bekynton 1443-65
Robert Stillington 1466-91
Richard Fox 1492-4
Oliver King 1495-1503
Hadrian de Castello 1504-18
Thomas Wolsey 1518-23
John Clerk 1523-41
William Knight 1541-7
William Barlow 1548-53
Gilbert Bourne 1554-9
Gilbert Berkerley 1560-81
Thomas Godwin 1584-90
John Still 1593-1608
James Montague 1608-16
Arthur Lake 1616-26
William Laud 1626-8
Leonard Mawe 1628-9
Walter Curll 1629-32
William Piers 1632-70
Robert Creyghton 1670-2
Peter Mews 1673-84
Thomas Kenn 1685-91
Richard Kidder 1691-1703
George Hooper 1703-27
John Wynne 1727-43
Edward Willes 1743-73
Charles Moss 1774-1802
Richard Beadon 1802-24
George Henry Law 1824-45
Richard Bagot 1845-54
Robert John Eden, Baron Auckland 1854-69
Lord Arthur Charles Hervey 1869-94
George Wyndham Kennion 1894-1921
St John Basil Wynne Wilson 1921-37
Francis Underhill 1937-43
John William Charles Wand 1943-5
Harold William Bradfield 1946-60
Edward Barry Henderson 1960-75
John Monier Bickersteth 1975-87
George Leonard Cary 1987-91
James Thompson 1991-2002
Peter Price 2002-

INDEX

Items in bold relate to illustrations or their captions